FIGHTING FOR WALES

For
Leopold Kohr

First impression: St.David's Day, 1991

© Y Lolfa Cyf., 1991

ISBN: 0 86243 236 7

Cover design by Marian Delyth

Printed and published in Wales by Y Lolfa Cyf.,
Talybont, Dyfed SY24 5HE; tel (0970 86) 304, fax 782.

FIGHTING FOR WALES

GWYNFOR EVANS

y Lolfa

Contents

Introduction

AT THE time of the formation of Plaid Genedlaethol Cymru (the Welsh Nationalist Party) by six people in 1925 Welsh political national consciousness had ceased to exist. Consequently in the inter-war decades, before the little party had gained any strength, not a single concession was made to Wales by central government. The existence of Welsh nationhood was not recognised by Whitehall and Westminster. If it were not for Plaid Cymru this position would have continued unchanged during the following generations with malign consequences for Welsh national life.

Although the English parties were so deeply-rooted the little nationalist party succeeded in establishing itself as the first independent Welsh party, a considerable feat. Even the war failed to destroy it. Its workers were few but their commitment to fighting for Wales was tough. For the first time ever Wales was the focus of all the political activity of an increasing number of men and women, in contrast to the five or ten per cent of their time given to Welsh national affairs by 'good Welshmen' in the English parties, most of whose members gave Wales no thought at all.

The party performed services essential to national survival. It kept alive the idea of Welsh nationhood as a political factor. It established the idea of Wales as a national entity in economic life. It put the idea of national freedom on the agenda. The Anglo British establishment and parties jibed at its smallness, yet their fear of its growth was shown by savagely rubbishing it as medieval and fascist, the supporter of totalitarian dictators of the right. They jeered ceaselessly at its weakness but they showed an increasing awareness of its potential. Nationalism is the one force in Wales that London governments respect. One concession after another was made in the post-war decades on the grounds, which the party had hammered into public consciousness, that Wales is a nation. The sum of these concessions is considerable. In 1978 an Act giving Wales an elected assembly was put on the Statute Book. It occasioned the biggest manifestation of people power in Welsh history. This did not carry the Welsh people forward to a Welsh democracy in the way people power has done so magnificently among the nations of the former Warsaw Pact and Baltic countries. Welsh people power was used in the 1979 referendum to hurl a tiny measure of freedom back in the government's face so that centralist English rule be safely reasserted in Wales.

Naturally London government contemptuously assumed that the Welsh had rejected the concept of a national future and that Welsh national opinion could be brushed aside. That is what it did with impunity during the next twelve years, with one major exception—the Welsh language television issue. Yet Welsh nationalism continued to be a creative force. It continued to invigorate national consciousness through electoral and non-electoral campaigns. For more than half a century it has fought campaigns to defend and strengthen Welsh life. The importance of the struggle is basic. It is the fight which has awakened the Welsh spirit, and what other party has fought for Wales? Each campaign has contributed a little to awakening and raising national consciousness. This is probably the party's most important contribution to national survival. It has helped for example to infuse Welsh national pride and consciousness in the scores of thousands of parents in the south-east of Wales who have sent their children to Welsh-medium schools although they have no Welsh themselves.

The main subject of this book is the non-electoral campaigns fought by Plaid Cymru to defend and strengthen Welsh life. Each one reflects the humiliating position of a subject nation, and each reveals something of the attitude of the Anglo British government and parties to Welsh nationhood. Each awakened or deepened a sense of national identity in some people. The questions are raised, what would the condition of Wales be today if there had been no party to fight for her? Would there be hope of a national future?

1 / Welsh Dimension Fades Out

IN THE immediate post-war years 1919-1922, nationalist movements achieved national freedom in Finland, Estonia, Latvia, Lithuania, Czechoslovakia, Jugoslavia and Ireland. Yet in Wales, where the historical, economic and cultural conditions for a flourishing autonomous life had been more favourable than in any of these countries, the movement was away from national freedom, and towards closer integration in England. There was no Welsh nationalist organisation and no sense of political loyalty to the nation. Political loyalty to Wales, which is the essence of Welsh nationalism, was almost non-existent. Far from achieving national freedom the Welsh had failed to create even a national party. Consequently, although the power of nationality as an organising principle has been demonstrated in scores of countries, Wales is not among them. It remains a nation without a government.

There had been a brief excursion into nationalist politics in the 1890's under the leadership of Lloyd George and Tom Ellis, who both, under the influence of Parnell, flirted with the idea of creating an independent national party. Nothing came of it. The Cymru Fydd movement remained firmly within the Liberal Party. Even so it had enough strength to compel the Prime Minister, Lord Rosebery, to declare his support for Welsh home rule in a speech in Cardiff in 1895. Tom Ellis ceased to fight for a parliament when he took a government office; he died at forty. Lloyd George and other Liberal leaders abandoned the struggle. Before his marriage to Margaret Owen Lloyd George had bluntly declared his motives in a letter to her. 'My supreme idea is to get on. To this I shall sacrifice everything—except, I trust, honesty. I am prepared to thrust even love itself under the wheels of my Juggernaut if it obstructs the way.' The home rule movement vanished from the land as completely as if it had never been.

The Welsh intelligentsia had long been possessed of a death-wish. From the middle forties of the 19th century on they had decided that the Welsh language and the Welsh nation had no future and should have none. In introducing the resolution in parliament which led to the appointment of the Royal Commission whose infamous report was known as The Treason of the Blue Books, William Williams of Llanpumsaint, M.P. for Coventry, encapsulated the attitude of the intellectuals:

> If the Welsh had the same advantages for education as the Scotch [sic], they would, instead of appearing as a distinct people, in no respect differ from the English.

This was the wish of most intellectuals, 'in no respect [to] differ from the English.' The English establishment reciprocated this wish. It was in this period that Engels observed,

> The English know how to reconcile people of the most diverse races with their rule. The Welsh, who held so tenaciously to their nationality and language, have fused completely with the British Empire.

How different was the situation in Finland and Estonia. Incorporated in Russia, they had no literature nor even a literary language until the middle of the 19th century. The mass of the people were serfs. But when the intellectuals of Wales, heirs to the oldest living literature in Europe, excepting Greek literature, were yielding to a death-wish, the former serfs of Finland and Estonia were stirred by the will to live a full and dignified national life. When the impetus for a national future, briefly channelled in the Cymru Fydd movement, exhausted itself, this deep Welsh malaise persisted and still finds expression in a myriad ways.

Although a Liberal government was returned with a massive majority in 1906, and not a single Conservative was elected in Wales, no step was taken towards self-government. With a very few exceptions Welsh Liberal nationalism was engulfed by an avalanche of offices and honours, and erstwhile Liberal nationalists were absorbed by Anglo-British politics, giving little more thought than the London establishment to a national future for Wales. With no political organisation to promote it, the future of the Welsh nation became a dead issue. Although there were numerous Irish and Scottish parliamentary measures in the pre-war years Welsh legislation was conspicuous by its absence. Sir Ben Bowen Thomas wrote:

> By the 1910 Parliament the Welsh Parliamentary Party had lost its chance of winning for Welsh affairs an undeniable and recognised place in British politics... Wales had become a collection of individual constituencies because the political ideal had now been shattered. When E.T.John rose on 11 March, 1914, to present his Self-government for Wales measure, the few who were there listened to his voice as to the cry of one risen from the dead.

Nevertheless Cymru Fydd nationalism bore fruit in the establishment of major national institutions, the National University, National Library, National Museum and the independent Church in Wales.

Between 1900 and 1920 the fragmentation of Wales went rapidly ahead. It was hastened by factors which would have been less injurious if the nation had had a government to give it cohesion. These included the decline of nonconformity, the class war and especially the Great War.

The war eliminated all thought of a national future, engulfing the people in a sea of emotional Anglo British-ness. 280,000 Welshmen, two-thirds of the country's male population between 20 and 40 years of age, served in the armed forces, a bigger proportion than in England or Scotland. Absorbed by millions of Englishmen in the English military system they were frequently even forbidden to write home in Welsh. When Lloyd George, the former Welsh nationalist leader, achieved dazzling power and glory as the the man who won the war, he weaned Welshmen's loyalty still further from Wales, as Henry Tudor had done centuries earlier, and fused them still more firmly in the aspirations of Greater England. Reared by a Llanystumdwy village cobbler, he was the greatest man in a state which emerged from the war immeasurably more powerful and centralised than ever before, powerful enough to destroy the Welsh nation merely by ignoring her existence.

Some small compensation for the disappearance of Liberal nationalism was found in the adoption by the growing Labour Party in 1918 of a policy of 'home rule all round' which had been advocated by its founder, Keir Hardie.

At that time Labour leaders had no shred of doubt about the value of self-government for Wales. This was expressed forcibly by Arthur Henderson:

> The Labour Party is pledged to the widest and most generous measure of home rule that can be devised... We regard the claims of Wales to self-government on these lines as strictly analogous to those of Ireland... Nationalism means the vigorous development of the material and moral resources of the whole people. It is hardly possible to conceive an area in which a scheme of parliamentary self-government could be established with better chances of success [than Wales]... Given self-government, Wales might establish itself as a modern utopia, and develop its own institutions, its own arts, its own culture, its own ideal of democracy in politics, industry and social life, as an example and an inspiration to the rest of the world.

These were not the over-enthusiastic words of a political lightweight, spoken to gain electoral advantage. They were the honest opinion of Labour's most experienced heavyweight. Arthur Henderson had been Labour's representative in Lloyd George's War Cabinet. He was, says A.J.P.Taylor, 'the leader of the most important Labour movement on the Allied side.' It was Henderson and Webb who devised the Labour Party policy in 1918, the year in which the words above were written. Arthur Henderson was generally expected to be Labour's first Prime Minister. He did become its first Foreign Secretary. His assessment of the value of self-government for Wales was the considered opinion of the foremost policy maker among Labour politicians at a time when Labour's judgement of the issue was still objective, unimpaired by the fear of self-government's effect on Labour's prospects of forming a government.

So far from becoming a utopia, within three years Wales sank into a hideous depression in which the proportion of unemployed men soared to 38 per cent, by far the worst in Europe. During the tragic inter-war years nearly half a million Welsh people were transferred to England under the policy of Transference of Labour, London's only answer to the Welsh crisis.

When it formed a minority government in 1923 it became clear to the Labour Party that its chance of forming governments in the future would be more than uncertain without the solid phalanx of Welsh Labour members on which to rely. Since their number would be reduced under home rule, support for the policy wilted. Although self-government would obviously be good for Wales it would not be good for the Labour Party. This is enough to explain the party's subsequent opposition to Welsh self-government. It bears no relation to the welfare of Wales. Even for Welsh Labour M.P's party interests take precedence over Welsh national interests, although self-government would have given Wales a radical government of the Left as regularly as Sweden.

The attempt to revive home rule activity after the war was pathetically irresolute and ineffectual. The final home rule conference held at Shrewsbury on 31 March 1922 was a fiasco. There was no movement to organise it. The fifty who attended were hopelessly at odds with each other. Self-government was a dead issue. The tactic of working for Wales through the Anglo British parties was exposed as a humiliating failure. It would not regain a semblance of credibility until the fear of nationalist political potential levered some concessions from the London parties. Without the support of organised nationalism the Welsh five per cent of Britain's population have no power to galvanise the British establishment into acting for Wales. Political nationalism is the only sanction Wales has. In its absence in the two inter-war decades Wales was given no more parliamentary attention than if it did not exist. There were many cultural nationalists in the Anglo British parties in those years, but none who gave their political loyalty to Wales, none who accepted responsibility before the world for their nation. Politically the Welsh dimension disappeared from sight.

In the post-war years the Welsh people appeared to be passively resigned to Wales remaining permanently a powerless peripheral region of England. National political consciousness seemed extinct. 'By 1922', says Hywel Davies, 'the distinctiveness of Welsh politics in terms of issues seemed to be at an end.' The Welsh dimension would not begin to reappear on the political agenda until nationalism showed potential for growth towards the end of the second world war. Nor was there evidence of militant Welshness in the cultural sphere; even cultural nationalism was anaemic. With national consciousness apparently destined to go into an unchecked decline the nation's demise seemed to be only a matter of time. The grim years of economic depression did nothing to prevent, but rather hastened, the relegation of Welsh nationhood to the sidelines as an irritating irrelevance. Rebuilding Welsh life on the basis of nationhood was thought a bizarre concept. Class loyalty was the order of the day in Wales; national loyalty was derided. There was no movement which tried to stop the rot, none with a vision of a future Wales. Welsh civilisation seemed doomed to die of apathy. An ancient nation seemed fated to perish without a fight.

The national decline would have continued unchecked but for the meeting of a laughably tiny group of six people in a Pwllheli café during the 1925 National Eisteddfod week. They formed the first and only independent Welsh political party, Plaid Genedlaethol Cymru—the Welsh Nationalist Party. Very small, but completely independent of the Anglo British parties, it would look at Wales and the world not through London but through Welsh eyes. Lewis Valentine was elected president for the first year, to be followed by Saunders Lewis who held the office for 13 years. Both were ex-servicemen, both had been wounded, and both had become nationalists while in the forces, Saunders Lewis largely under Irish influence. 'Through reading the literature of Yeats, Synge, Patrick Colum,' he said, 'it was through these that I came for the first time to realise what patriotism and the spirit of a nation are.'

A decade after its foundation Lloyd George, in a National Eisteddfod speech at Fishguard, scornfully compared the little party with Jonah's gourd, 'which came up in a night and perished in a night.' It was the once mighty Liberal Party however that came close to perishing. The tiny Welsh party did indeed face a desperate struggle for survival. Its task was immense, its resources insignificant. It had to fight on two fronts, against the Anglo British establishment in London but in Wales also, for the mass of Welsh people were strongly opposed to the idea of national freedom. When the Irish and other nations of the British

Empire fought for national freedom they had their own people at their back; not so in Wales. Nor could the circumstances of the first two decades of the party's existence have been more unpropitious, first the devastating economic depression and then total war. Consequently, in the Carmarthen constituency in 1945 there were only a dozen members and not a single branch. The first branch was formed in Gwynfe, Llangadog, in 1946 after a county council election which I lost by one vote. In that year Wynne Samuel was the only nationalist to win a local council seat in the party name. Nevertheless seven parliamentary seats were fought in the 1945 general election as well as two by-elections. Deposits were lost in every seat fought in general elections. The party's defeats are numbered in hundreds, its victories are few. But in Pilsudski's words, 'To be defeated, and not to give in, is victory.'

If the party had not continued to fight against all the odds it is unlikely that our vulnerable little nation would have survived the 20th century's traumatic economic and political, social, cultural and demographic pressures with real hope of a national future.

2 / British Nationalism Versus Welsh Nationalism

THE IDEA of full national status for Wales stirs deep and hostile emotions. Welsh nationalism has been anathema even among Welsh people, reviled with a loathing once evoked by Irish nationalism. Small nation nationalism elsewhere in the world excites little or no antipathy in the British breast. Scores are warmly approved. Nobody has a critical word for the vigorous nationalisms of the Scandinavian countries, and few outside Russia speak ill of the militant nationalism of the Baltic countries. Mandela's nationalism and Namibian nationalism in South Africa are applauded. But when Welsh nationalism could not be ignored it has been the butt of splenetic attacks.

This is not because of the especially evil nature of Welsh nationalism, which is moderate and civilised, peaceful and nonviolent. It arouses hostility because it threatens the existence of the United Kingdom of Great Britain and Northern Ireland, and in Wales in addition touches the Welsh conscience. The quite irrational malevolence shown towards it, now ebbing strongly, is given emotional force by Anglo British nationalism, the only nationalism found in Wales before the establishment of Plaid Cymru. The struggle in Wales is between two nationalisms, Welsh nationalism and the Anglo British state nationalism, the immense moral power which suffocates Welsh nationhood and the emotive force behind the Anglo British state. Euphemistically called patriotism it is often indistinguishable from great-nation chauvinism. It is markedly different from the moderate nonviolent nationalism of Wales, which simply aims to achieve the status which will enable the Welsh nation to live a full national life in freedom, taking her due place in the international order. When Plaid Cymru was established British nationalism had long been a powerful political force in Wales, but the only kind of Welsh nationalism was a vapid cultural nationalism.

Full national status will give this old and talented nation power of control over its domestic life, including military expenditure, and enable it to contribute to international life through the European Community, the United Nations and other international institutions. If this status had been achieved when Finland ceased to be incorporated in the Russian Empire after the first world war the strength and vigour of Welsh national life might compare with Finland's today.

Welsh nationalism has always rejected the idea of absolute sovereignty. Its aim has been to achieve the degree of freedom necessary to full national life. It demanded political freedom in the context of economic interdependence. When its constitutional policy was framed in the early thirties this was defined as dominion status. British dominions were, in the words of the Statute of Westminster, 'free and equal nations, in no way subordinate one to the other in any aspect of their domestic or external affairs.' They freely cooperated as members of the British Commonwealth of Nations. The goal which dominion status made possible was close partnership with the countries of Britain in a confederation of free and equal nations. Ireland could have entered such a confederation, incidentally solving the intractable Northern Irish problem. Fianna Fail showed enough interest in the concept in the late 40's to organise a meeting which I addressed in the National University in Dublin. A Britannic Confederation would be similar to the Nordic Council with joint boards to ensure common legislation, but the cooperation between the entities would of course be closer still. Well before the creation of the European Common Market, Plaid Cymru advocated a Britannic Confederation in which there would be no tariffs, tolls or passports. People, capital and goods would move as freely between the countries of the Confederation as they do today.

This civilised policy was of course dismissed out of hand as unthinkable. It would be the end of the huge Great British state, and it opened the nightmarish prospect for Anglo British nationalists of all parties of the final disappearance of British Greatness, which was a main concern of British parties. After Labour's disastrous defeat by the SNP in Govan, George Robertson, Labour M.P. for neighbouring Hamilton, rallied the party by declaring in the *Sunday Times* that, unlike the SNP, the Labour Party is 'no less interested than the Tories in keeping Britain "great"'. The devotion of the Anglo British parties to the dream of British Greatness is a deep chasm between them and the Welsh and Scottish national parties.

In considering British nationalism the basic distinction between nation and state must be kept in mind. Britishness is essentially a matter of statehood. Great Britain is a state, a multinational state, miscalled a nation-state. The word state is a euphemism to describe the apparatus controlled by bureaucrats and politicians, the instrument of the ruling group, located mainly in London. Diminishing the power of the state over Wales and her people would reduce the influence of Whitehall and Westminster over them. This is the meaning of decentralisation of power—transferring the power of London bureaucrats and politicians to the people of Wales. It will happen when the Welsh people will it to happen. The power of the Anglo British state in Wales rests on the will of the Welsh people. Since will and not force is the basis of the state, it will cease when the Welsh people will to take over responsibility for their life.

The British state however has usurped the concept of

nation. Its emotional hold over the people of the countries of Britain derives from the notion, sedulously promoted by the establishment, of British nationhood, powerfully symbolised by the crown. The idea of a British nation was first conceived during the Napoleonic wars, 1793-1815, since when British nationalism has dominated and marginalised Wales. It ripened quickly with the threat of French invasion. A regiment did land at Fishguard in 'the last invasion of Britain', to be frightened into surrender by Jemima Nicholas' army of women in their Welsh red petticoats and black hats. This farcical incident itself accelerated the war's identification of the Welsh people with England/Britain. War, including the 78 wars fought by Britain in the last century and especially the great wars of this century, has been one of the two major factors in the growth of British state nationalism. The other is the British Empire, whose glory dazzled the Welsh. The association of British nationalism with war and empire has given it a militarist and imperialist character. The extent of popular support for the Suez and Falkland wars illustrates its nature. Power hungry and with a yearning for greatness it has no cultural content. Unlike Welsh and other moderate small nation nationalisms, it does not recognise the rights and democratic aspirations of all other national, language, ethnic and minority groups world-wide.

The function of a state is to serve the nation in a subordinate capacity. If it performs its function well the nation grows in health and strength. The British state has a group of nations to serve, of which England is overwhelmingly the biggest. 83% of the population of Great Britain live in England, only 5% in Wales. The consequence of English predominance is that the British state is run in the interests of England. Far from serving the Welsh nation in a subordinate role its domination of Wales has been entire, so that a nation of enormous possibilities is in a state of ruin. Ever since the English parliament's 1536 Act of Incorporation declared Wales to be 'incorporated, united and annexed and subject to' to England (there was no Britain then), the Anglo British state has been by far the most powerful agency eroding Welsh nationhood. It was statutes of the English parliament which excluded the Welsh language from Welsh legal and official life; which excluded monoglot Welsh-speaking people from all public offices in an age when Wales was as monoglot Welsh-speaking as England was monoglot English-speaking; which expelled J.P.'s from the bench if they spoke Welsh in the course of their duties; which abolished Welsh law and destroyed the Welsh legal system; and which imposed a wholly English system of education on Wales in which children were punished if they spoke to each other in Welsh in school. It was the state Church of England which for 150 years in the 17th and 18th centuries filled every Welsh bishopric with monoglot English bishops. It was the state which failed to build an infrastructure to serve Wales so that we still have no major north-south road to unite the country and help to counter unemployment and depopulation. Typically, demands over two generations for major north-south highways, as from Cardiff to Wrexham and Swansea to Caernarfon, have been rejected for unacknowledged political reasons, to keep Wales divided in accordance with the classic policy of divide and rule. It was the British state which presided over unemployment when it reached the appalling figure of 38 per cent, by far the worst in Europe, and which introduced the policy of Transference of Labour as its only solution. It is a state which has never tried to create a balanced Welsh economy but has been content to see our rich resources exploited to the point of exhaustion and our people emigrate to England by the hundred thousand in search of work. It has never produced a comprehensive policy to strengthen and restore the splendid language spoken in Wales since the post-Roman years. Such is the service the Anglo British state has given the nation of Wales.

The use of the word British to include English, Scots, Welsh and Irish (northern Irish only since 1921) is a recent development. Prys Morgan has pointed out that up to the 18th century the British were the Welsh. The English were English, the Scots Scots, the Irish Irish, but the Welsh, as well as being called Welsh (the name given by Germanic peoples to those who had been under Roman rule) were also called Britons or Cambro-Britons. It was only after the union between England and Scotland in 1707, 1200 years after the Age of Saints when a Welsh national community came into being, that the English government adopted the term British to camouflage the state's English character and to weaken the Scots, Irish and Welsh sense of distinct national identity. The small nations were no longer simply Scots, Irish and Welsh; they were also British, regarded as sub-nations with a dual nationality. For the English people, more than four-fifths of the population of the British state, who are the people of the state as the Russians are the people of the state in the Russian empire, the idea of England as a sub-nation has never been other than ludicrous, although that is the logical consequence of asserting that Britain is a nation. There is no dichotomy for English people. For them the British 'nation' is the English nation writ large.

The United Kingdom, Nairn's Ukania, is a state not a nation, a huge highly centralised power state which has 37 times the population of Estonia but only one government. It is the most highly centralised and least democratic state in the European Community. Switzerland with a tenth of the UK's population has 27 governments, but no more than one nation. The United Kingdom has distinct Celtic nations as well as England within its border. It was in order to maintain the cohesion of this multinational structure that the state was dressed in the guise of nationhood. A policy of confusing state and nation in the public mind was assiduously pursued. Politicians, the establishment and the media unceasingly speak of the British state as 'this nation of ours'. The degrading of Scots, Irish and Welsh nationality and the pretence of British nationhood, have been the necessary condition of maintaining the multi-national United Kingdom as a unitary 'nation-state'. The fear which haunts Anglo British nationalists is the achievement of full national status by the Scots and the Welsh, for if that is won the British state will cease to be; Great Britain will go out of history. And if the British state ceases to exist, where will the 'British nation' be then? States come and go, but nations remain; they do not disappear with the loss of statehood. Nations can survive without a state, as Wales has done up to now. Great Britain however is a state only. If it were also a nation its nationhood would survive the state's dissolution. But obviously when Wales and Scotland as well as England enjoy full statehood one could not speak of a British nation. Like the Soviet nation the 'British nation' is an abstract nation. But whereas the idea of Soviet nationhood has now collapsed the concept of British nationhood is incessantly promoted.

If there is no British nation, what is Britishness? Is there a difference between British culture and English culture? Apart from geography and the state, are not things British English? British literature is English literature. The British language is the English language. The British constitution is the English constitution. The British Crown is the English Crown, the British parliament the English parliament. And as A.J.P.Taylor has said, with the first world war, 'the history of the English state and of the English people merged for the first time.' In Anthony Sampson's 731 page study of the British power structure, *The Anatomy of Britain,* there is not a single reference to Wales, and all the Scottish references amount to no more than a couple of score lines. For Sampson, as for English people and government, Britain is England writ large.

'For the English', says Anthony Barnett, 'to be English is

to be English; to be British is to be English in the world.'
For Churchill the English were 'this island race', echoing
Shakespeare's bit about 'this scepter'd isle', which incident-
ally was written half a century after Wales was incor-
porated in England. The historian G.M.Trevelyan saw
England as 'a strange island anchored off the continent.'
English people make little distinction between England and
Britain. They certainly don't merge their national identity in
a British 'national' consciousness. Indeed Fowler's *Modern
English Usage* says,

> It must be remembered that no Englishman calls him-
> self a Briton without a sneaking sense of the ludic-
> rous... The most that can be expected (of an
> Englishman) is... that when Scots and others are
> likely to be within earshot *Britain* and *British* should
> be inserted as tokens, but no more, of what is really
> meant.

British and English nationalism have identical aims. In
his *Political Integration and Disintegration in the British
Isles* Anthony Birch defines English nationalism as, 'The
determination of the English to maintain the independence,
power and welfare of the British state they have created
and dominated.' This is the nationalism of Margaret
Thatcher and Neil Kinnock, but whereas Kinnock calls it
patriotism Thatcher is more open. 'I am an English
nationalist and never you forget it', she told a Scottish
Tory who favoured a measure of self-government for
Scotland. One is more shrill than the other but both are
nationalists. Tory nationalism is never wholly free from
jingo chauvinism. Welsh annual Conservative conferences
are concluded by singing Land of Hope and Glory:

> Wider still, and wider, may thy bounds be set;
> God who made thee mighty make thee mightier yet.

Neil Kinnock illustrated the admirable nature of his
nationalism by declaring to the Labour Conference that he
would be prepared to die for his country. How many

Welsh nationalists are prepared to die for Wales? On an election television programme he confided to the public that he would no more allow anyone to lay a finger on his country than on his family. To proclaim willingness to die for The United Kingdom of Great Britain and Northern Ireland would be a giggle; the full name of the state lacks resonance. Even to declare that no one shall lay a finger on Great Britain would be a bit of a laugh. Yet the epithet Great is a key to understanding British nationalism.

There are as many nationalisms as there are nations. No two are exactly alike. Some are vicious and virulent, others benign and benevolent. Welsh and British nationalism are radically different. The small nation nationalism of Wales is wholly pacific. It has no more threatened anyone than has Icelandic or Norwiegian nationalism. The great nation nationalism of Great Britain on the other hand has a long history of militarism and imperialism in which scores of lands and peoples have been threatened and attacked. Some, like the Tasmanian people, have been wiped out by it. Many wars have been fought by Great Britain, such as the Opium War to impose the sale of opium on China, to further its economic interests; others have been waged to sustain its imperial greatness.

British Greatness, commonly expressed in military symbols and pride in military prowess, bloomed in the time of the naval and military victories of Nelson and Wellington in the Napoleonic wars. Yearning for Greatness characterises the nationalisms of the Anglo British parties. It was to enhance Britain's Greatness that the Attlee government built the first British nuclear bomb. The function of the British bomb is not to defend; for that purpose it is useless. Its function is to give Great Britain the status of a great nuclear power. The same motive impelled Callaghan's government in 1976 to double the power of Polaris with the £1000 million Chevaline programme. The bomb is the badge of British nationalism. Today's most potent symbol of British Greatness is Trident, which is being built with the support of all the Anglo British parties despite the collapse of the Warsaw Pact. The British thirst for Greatness drives Great Britain, despite its comparative poverty, to spend a considerably higher proportion of its budget on armaments than the average for EEC countries, and three times as much as Finland which shares a 778 mile frontier with Russia. Even though the Cold War has ended, all the structures of militarism still exist. Great Britain still has nuclear weapons, it is still 'modernising' these weapons. The nature of British nationalism thus prevents Great Britain from adjusting to its post-imperial role. The longing for Greatness keeps breaking in. Welsh nationalists applaud John Seymour's sentiment: 'I don't want to live in a *great* country. I want to live in a civilised one.'

The ostensible reason for Great Britain's colossal military expenditure is to maintain the state's independence, the fundamental tenet of British nationalism. This was the aim which inspired Gaitskell's nationalistic appeal to a thousand years of British history (which would take one back to the Danish conquest nearly eight centuries before Great Britain came into existence) in support of his opposition to British entry into the Common Market. The Labour left's nationalism was manifested in its strong opposition to subservience to the U.S., which it said reduced Britain to colonial status. Their cry for independence came from the heart. But significantly the Left has never supported, still less promoted, the principle of Welsh and Scottish independence. Even the Communist Party of Great Britain shared this nationalist determination to maintain Britain's independence. Palme Dutt, its leading theoretician for a generation, declared, 'We demand the national independence of the British people', and he spoke up against 'The American penetration and domination. . . directed against Britain', and of 'the struggle for liberation'. Welsh nationalists too struggle for liberation. Their struggle, free though it is from militarism and imperialism, is derided, whereas the British nationalist determination to maintain Britain's independence and greatness, through violent methods if thought necessary, is considered wholly admirable. It is against this immensely powerful British nationalism, which has so deeply infected their compatriots, that Welsh nationalists struggle for national liberation.

3 / The Burning of the Bombing School

IN THE absence of a potentially strong nationalist party in the inter-war years Welsh national needs and opinion were despised by the London establishment. Not a single concession of value was made by government to Welsh opinion in the two decades. Government's disdainful insensibility was displayed by its decision to plant an RAF bombing school in the heart-land of Welsh-speaking Llŷn. This brutal example of how the language and culture of a vulnerable little nation were assailed by the government responsible for their protection takes its place in recent Welsh annals with the devastation of Epynt and the drowning of Cwm Tryweryn. It occurred in 1936, on the fourth centenary of the 1536 Act of Incorporation by which England 'incorporated, united and annexed' Wales. The heroic response of three nationalists to this act of government aggression was a seminal event in Welsh politics. Although few took part it was nevertheless an insurrection, the first since the days of Owain Glyndŵr. A full account is found in Dafydd Jenkins' *Tân yn Llŷn,* on which I have relied heavily in this chapter.

Countries determined to prevent another suicidal war came together in the World Disarmament Conference in Geneva in February 1932. Foreseeing the limitless destruction which bombing from the air would cause among civilians the representatives of Germany and Italy, Russia, Japan and the USA recommended the abolition of bombing planes. Dr.Beneš, prime minister of Czechoslovakia, was requested to prepare a report on the matter. On its receipt the Conference resolved to eliminate bombing from the air. One great power alone opposed the resolution. Lord Londonderry, Air Minister in Ramsay Macdonald's government, insisted on Great Britain's right to bomb from the air in defence of its Empire. Although Anthony Eden, the foreign secretary, could rally only three countries to support the Great British stand, Iraq, Persia (Iran) and Siam (Thailand), this was enough to scupper the proposal to ban aerial bombing.

Soon afterwards the British government embarked on a huge rearmament programme in which the air force had a prominent place. In presenting the plans to the the House of Lords Lord Londonderry said,

> In 1932 the Disarmament Conference assembled, and almost its earliest discussions were centred around the possibility of the total abolition of Air Forces, or at least the abolition of the artillery of the air, the bombing plane, which is the weapon which is the distinctive arm of the Air Force and to which it owes its separate existence... I had the utmost difficulty at the time, amid the public outcry, in preserving the use of the bombing plane...

It was as an item in the rearmament programme that the Under Secretary for Air announced in the House of Commons in May 1935 that,

> proposals are under consideration for the establishment of an armament training camp and an aerodrome in connection therewith at Hell's Mouth (Porth Neigwl) in Carnarvonshire.

The announcement was seen by Welsh nationalists as a challenge. Professor J.E.Daniel, the nationalist candidate in Caernarfonshire in the 1935 general election, put the bombing school proposal in its military context:

> Let Wales remember that this aerodrome is but a part of the general policy of rearmament. If Wales wants to protest effectively against it, she must protest against the policy of which it is a part.

The purpose of the establishment, to teach the art of aerial bombing, was one of the two main grounds for opposition throughout the campaign. Its object was not to defend the life of Wales but to defend imperial frontiers and to attack the towns of England's enemies. Baldwin had declared in the House of Commons on 12 November 1932, before Hitler took power, when Germany was still a friendly democracy,

> The only defence is attack. That means that you must kill women and children more quickly than the enemy if yours are to be saved.

To train men in that hideous craft was the purpose of the bombing school. Saunders Lewis prophesied that,

> The main targets of the bombing planes in the next war will be the great cities of enemy countries, to burn and poison them, to turn the civilization of centuries to dust, to hurl down from the safety of the air the most cruel death on women and children and unarmed and defenceless men.

A true prophecy. Aerial bombing was omnipresent in the war; it caused the death of a substantial proportion of the 32 million civilians who were killed between 1939 and 1945. 387 were killed by German bombers in Swansea, 620 in Coventry. In Hamburg 40,000 were killed in one night, and in two consecutive nights in September 1944, 120,000 were burnt and bombed to death in Dresden, one of Europe's most beautiful cities, chosen for this treatment because it was full of refugees fleeing before the Soviet armies. 80,000 people were killed in a single attack on Tokyo, and in the following three months a quarter of the citizens of numerous Japanese cities were killed before nuclear aerial bombing obliterated Hiroshima and Nagasaki. Nine years had elapsed since the Fire in Llŷn.

By burning the buildings of the bombing school three great Welshmen cried NO to bombing from the air. The year before the fire 80 per cent of the electors of Caernarfonshire had voted in the great Peace Ballot for the abolition of aerial bombing, but the government rode as roughly over domestic opinion as it did over international opinion.

Saunders Lewis noted the influence of armament makers—Merchants of Death as they were called at the time—on the government's determination to adhere to aerial bombing. Sir Harry McGowan, Chairman of ICI, justified the practice, adding for good measure, 'I have no objection to selling arms to both sides. I am not a purist in these things.' Since then the British government, now second in the world arms sales league, has zealously followed the same policy.

Lavish expenditure on arms was contrasted by Saunders Lewis with the government's churlish attitude to the wretched of the Welsh earth. Over a hundred babes and small children in Merthyr Tydfil suffered from severe rheumatism. This, like the distressing condition of pregnant mothers, was a consequence of the appalling housing and the low standard of sustenance of the Merthyr poor during the decades of devastating depression. A generous citizen offered the Merthyr Education Committee a large house for conversion into a school and hospital for the rheumatic little ones. When the Committee applied for a grant of £30,000 to enable them to implement the scheme the government forbade them to accept the gift. The issue of the newspaper which carried the story of the government's response also reported the initial cost of the Llŷn bombing school. It was £300,000.

The purpose of the bombing school was one of the two main grounds of opposition. The other was its intrusion, together with an accompanying English colony, into the peace, beauty and rich culture of a wholly Welsh-speaking neighbourhood. The Llŷn peninsula, through which the ancient Pilgrims' Way ran to the holy isle of Bardsey, was one of the few remaining homes of pure Welsh idiom and native culture. One cannot calculate, said Saunders Lewis, the irreparable loss to a language of purity of idiom, of a home of literature, of a tradition of Welsh civilisation reaching back fourteen hundred years. These things have no price. Llŷn, which was Welsh of the Welsh, was irreplaceable in the nation's life. The old house of Penyberth, which was pulled down a week before the sheds were burnt, had been a resting place in the Middle Ages for pilgrims on their way to Ynys Enlli (Bardsey), the Isle of Saints. The tradition is that twenty thousand saints are buried there, including some of the most famous such as Beuno, Dyfrig and Padarn. In his court speech Saunders Lewis claimed that if the moral law counted for anything the people who should be in the dock were the vandals responsible for the destruction of Penyberth. The bombing school illustrated the threat posed by the state to the whole future of the Welsh tradition.

Local and national opposition mounted. More than five thousand Llŷn people signed a petition opposing the bombing school. 1,500 societies and religious bodies, representing half a million people throughout Wales, voiced their protest. Every Welsh writer and poet of stature, and every Welsh language periodical, supported the nationalist opposition. The Roman Catholic Church was prominent among the opponents. The *Catholic Herald* considered it a duty of the Church to identify itself with the growing nationalism in Wales. 'One thing is quite certain,' it said, 'if the Catholic Church in Wales allies itself boldly (as it has done in history) with the legitimate demands of nationalist sentiment and culture, then nothing can bar its way.' Archbishop Mihangel McGrath pressed the Prime Minister to receive a deputation from Wales to discuss the matter.

The demand for a deputation was supported by many of the most prominent Welsh people of the day. Nevertheless it was rejected by the government. *The Times* even refused to publish a letter from leaders of Welsh life. Like the radio issue, this reflected the contemptuous attitude of the government and establishment towards Wales in the thirties, an attitude which would have probably continued and deteriorated further but for the rise of political nationalism. Two bombing schools were to have been established in England, one in the south, the other in the north. Near Abbotsbury, the southern site, a breeding ground for swans was the reason for strong protests in *The Times* and other establishment papers. The Ministry withdrew the plan. The northern location was near Holy Island in Northumberland. English scholars and writers, led by the historian G.M.Trevelyan, protested that it was outrageous to place a bombing school in an area which had historical associations with Lindisfarne and St.Cuthbert and where wild duck nested. The case appealed strongly to the London bureaucrats who shared the culture of the protestors. The Air Ministry summoned a special conference to consider the matter. Again it withdrew.

Saunders Lewis, Lewis Valentine and D.J.Williams decided to act. They were no ordinary men. Saunders Lewis, a university lecturer, was a scholar and poet, novelist and dramatist, the finest journalist and literary critic Wales has seen. Lewis Valentine, a Baptist minister, was the first president of Plaid Cymru and the first to stand in its name in a parliamentary election. A scholar and poet, he was wounded like Saunders Lewis in the first world war, from which he emerged a nationalist and a pacifist. D.J.Williams was for years a collier before graduating from the universities of Wales and Oxford. His volumes of autobiography, essays and short stories will be read as long as the Welsh language is read. All three were profound Christians. Saunders Lewis had expressed the conviction of the three in seeing nationalism as,

> a fountain head of heroism and brave resolve. . .
> There is nothing like the sense of belonging to a noble
> country and to courageous ancestors for inspiring
> youth to heroism.

That was the spirit in which the three acted, impelled by a passionate love of Wales, believing that a heavy term of imprisonment would be the inevitable consequence.

On 7 September 1936 they set fire to the sheds that had replaced Penyberth, taking care that nobody would be injured. In that sense it was a nonviolent act. Then, at about 2.30 a.m., they gave themselves up to the police in Pwllheli. They asked to see the Superintendent to whom they gave a letter for the Chief Constable confessing their responsibility and giving their motives. While the Superintendent went to the scene of the fire the three discussed Welsh literature. Williams Parry's sonnets were the subject. One said that Y Llwynog (The Fox) was his favourite. He began to recite it but his memory failed him. The recitation was completed by the police constable sitting nearby.

The trial was held in Caernarfon on 13 October. Dafydd Jenkins described the entry of the judge, Sir Wilfred Lewis, his great wig reaching to his shoulders, preceded by his retinue, including his chaplain in his degree gown and the sheriff, Mr.Armstrong-Jones, father of Lord Snowdon, attired in knee breeches with sword on thigh. The Commission was read, beginning 'Edward the Eighth, by the Grace of God, of Great Britain, Ireland and the British Dominions beyond the seas, King, Defender of the Faith...' The Clerk of the Court called the names of the twelve jurymen, including David Jones of Wônffor (Waunfawr) and John Aalec (Harlech) Jones.

The three were called to the dock and the indictment was read to each in turn accusing each that he had 'maliciously set fire to certain buildings belonging to His Majesty the King.' Dafydd Jenkins records the exchanges. Saunders Lewis was asked, 'How say you John Saunders Lewis, are you guilty or not guilty?'

S.L. 'Yr wyf yn ddieuog'. (I am not guilty)

Judge: 'Is John Saunders Lewis the person who is described in the indictment as a lecturer?'

S.L.	'Ie, darlithydd wyf fi, yn llenyddiaeth Cymru, yng Ngholeg y Brifysgol, Abertawe.' (Yes, I am a lecturer, in Welsh literature, in the University College, Swansea).
Judge,	more vociferously, 'Listen to me. Do you tell me that you cannot speak or understand English?'
S.L.	'Mi fedraf Saesneg, ond Cymraeg yw fy mamiaith'. (I can speak English but Welsh is my mother tongue.)
Judge,	with the emphasis of a cross-examining magistrate, 'Do you tell me that you cannot understand or speak English?'
S.L.	'Yr wyf yn gofyn yn ostyngedig i'm harglwydd ganiatáu imi ateb yn Gymraeg, am mai hi yw fy mamiaith. Gofynnaf i'r cyfieithydd gyfieithu hwn'. (I humbly ask my lord to permit me to answer in Welsh, because that is my mother tongue. I ask the interpreter to translate this).
Judge,	again: 'Do you understand and speak English?'
S.L.	'Yes my lord.'
Judge:	'Well then, you will plead to the indictment in English.'

The indictment was read a second time in English and Saunders Lewis was again asked in English if he pleaded guilty or not guilty.

S.L.	'Yr wyf yn ddieuog.' (I am not guilty)
Judge	'I will give you one more chance. Do you speak and understand English?'
S.L.	'Under protest then, my lord, I say that I plead not guilty.'

After going through the same rigmarole Lewis Valentine and D.J.Williams pleaded not guilty in English under protest. The defendants thus underlined the grossly inferior status of the national language of Wales, which had been described in the infamous 1847 Commission Report as 'only the language of perjury.'

Saunders Lewis and Lewis Valentine had no counsel, but D.J.Williams' counsel, Edmund Davies, now Lord Justice, challenged five of the jurors on account of their inability to speak Welsh. This angered the judge, who cried out after the third challenge, 'How long is this farce going on?'

In his brilliant address to the court Saunders Lewis pleaded that no state has a right to use another nation merely as a means of benefiting itself and that no state has a right to seek national advantages which do genuine harm to another nation. It was only after exhausting all legal means of restraining the English government's behaviour, he said, that the three had resolved to act.

> We determined on an action that would proclaim our conviction that the building of this bombing range in Llŷn is by all Christian principles wrong and unlawful. We resolved on an act that would compel the English government to take action at law against us... We ourselves were the first to give the authorities warning of the fire, and we proclaimed to them our responsibility. We made absolutely sure that no human life would be endangered.

The jury failed to agree. Yet no second trial was held in Caernarfon or anywhere else in Wales. The case was transferred to London. When Lloyd George heard that that the Old Bailey was to be the venue of the second trial he wrote to his daughter Megan:

> They crumble up when faced by Hitler or Mussolini, but they take it out of the smallest country in the realm, which they misgovern. This is a cowardly way of showing their strength through bullying... They run away from anyone powerful enough to stand up to them and take it out of the weak...This is the first government that has tried to put Wales on trial in the Old Bailey... I wish I were there... I certainly wish I were forty years younger.

Only once before in England had a case been moved to London after the failure of a jury to agree. In that exceptional case, Rex V Barrett, where the jury had been interferred with, the circumstances were wholly different. At the end of 1988 the British government tried to get Father Desmond Ryan extradited from Ireland to be tried in London. The Irish government refused on the grounds that he would not get a fair trial in London where he would not be tried by his peers and where his conviction by an English jury would be certain. So it was in the case of Saunders Lewis, Lewis Valentine and D.J.Williams. Robert Richards M.P. asked the Solicitor General in the House of Commons if he thought, "that these three Welshmen are likely to find their peers on the slopes of Ludgate Hill?" As in the case of Father Ryan the Minister replied that he resented the suggestion that a fair trial would not be obtained. In the event, when the Judge asked the jury to consider their verdict they did not bother to retire. Within seconds the foreman pronounced their verdict, 'Guilty'.

Sentenced to nine months imprisonment the three spent the term in Wormwood Scrubs. Their imprisonment re-established a tradition which had fallen into desuetude in Wales for over five centuries, that of resisting oppression and taking the consequences. Suffering imprisonment in the cause of Wales had been unknown in modern times. Since then scores of members of Plaid Cymru and at least a thousand members of Cymdeithas yr Iaith (The Welsh Language Society) have been imprisoned for acting in defence of Wales and her language, some for longer terms than the Penyberth three.

15,000 people packed Caernarfon's huge Eisteddfod Pavilion to welcome the three home on their release. This seemed to augur well for a Welsh national future. Their sacrifice, it appeared, was not in vain. But it soon became clear that the mass of Welsh people were unmoved. The *Western Mail* mirrored Welsh servility in its savage attack on the Caernarfon meeting as 'an orgy of crazed sentiment and absurd self-adulation.' Reflecting the hysterical hatred of pacific Welsh nationalism it accused D.J.Williams of all people of echoing Hitler. The sacking of Saunders Lewis by Swansea University College indicated the mood of the mass; for 15 years he was without a post, scraping a living by journalism and occasional lecturing. When Wales was swallowed by war two years later the defence of the nation was confined to a tiny minority.

Yet the burning of the bombing school is one of the high points in modern Welsh history. For the first time in centuries men had acted, not just talked, in the defence of the nation. Before Plaid Cymru was established Welsh-speaking communities had been destroyed without a fight at Llanwddyn when Liverpool built the huge Lake Vyrnwy reservoir and at Claerwen in the Elan Valley when Birmingham built its reservoirs there. But at Penyberth persons of stature had sacrificed their freedom in the nation's cause and had faced obloquy and persecution. This shook the British dream world, albeit temporarily, in which the Welsh had so long been contentedly cocooned. The impact on Welsh literature was profound, inaugurating a splendid new era in Welsh poetry. Hundreds began to think independently as Welsh people and to see the world through Welsh eyes. The fire helped to purge Welsh patriotism of sentimentality and to foster a sense of responsible Welsh citizenship. Its effect persists among patriots of all ages.

4 / War-time Witness: Rape of Epynt

AFTER FOURTEEN years of existence the national party was still very small when the second world war began. Known in Gwynedd as Y Blaid Bach, the Little Party, Caernarfonshire was the only parliamentary seat it had fought apart from the University of Wales seat, and it had only one member in its name on any local council. Hywel Davies contends in his book *The Welsh Nationalist Party 1925-1945* that its title

> proved to be a misnomer which predated the appearance of a nationalist *political party* by at least twenty years... The Nationalist Party during the 1920's and 1930's proved to be little more than an educational/cultural movement.

Outside the party it was generally assumed that it would not survive the war. Even Saunders Lewis doubted its survival. For although its opposition to Hitler and Nazism was total the party had the temerity to refuse to throw itself behind the British war effort. Giving its loyalty to Wales it considered its duty to be to defend the Welsh nation rather than the British state.

In the 19th century only such rare individual persons as Michael D.Jones had been critical of Britain's imperialistic militarism and the 78 wars which had resulted from it. A minority only supported Lloyd George's courageous opposition to the Boer War. 288,000 Welshmen joined the forces in the first world war, two-thirds of all men in the 20-40 age group, the highest proportion in any nation in Britain. Yet although that war was ostensibly fought by

Great Britain in defence of small nations there was no hint of defending the national life of Wales. On the contrary, perhaps it did more injury to Welsh life than a German invasion would have done. In the total war circumstances of 1914-18 the saturation of Welsh life by England and Englishness, and its manipulation by the Anglo British state, was total and was wholly unresisted. This was the situation which persisted throughout the post-war years. For a quarter of a century the fact of Welsh nationhood was utterly disregarded in the policies of the Anglo British parties.

This was the background to the Welsh nationalists' war-time stand for Wales. Their stance was utterly disgraceful in the eyes of the vast majority. But although many thought that to defend the Welsh nation when the British state was at war was a scandal verging on high treason, it was a duty that nationalists could not avoid. They knew that a flood of emotional Britishness would swamp Wales, weakening the sense of national identity, and that the harsher grip of the London establishment, for whom Wales was no more than a geographical expression, would speed the erosion of the fragile nation, while government resources would be mobilised in defence of English life.

The national party's position was stated in a conference called immediately after the outbreak of war in Caernarfon, its heartland. From the chair the Rev.Lewis Valentine declared that the party's duty was 'to see that Wales did not cease to exist.' The party President, Professor J.E.Daniel, said that, 'Although Wales is not regarded as a separate entity by England, and although its nationality is not respected, we are asked to sacrifice everything for the war effort.' Two resolutions were adopted:

(1) That this conference, firmly believing that nothing but evil can come to Wales through this war, requests the Government to call an armistice and a peace conference without delay.

(2)   That we ask the Government, in so far as it professes
to be fighting for the freedom and rights of small
nations and national minorities, to regard and respect
Wales as a nation, and acknowledge that fact in three
ways:
(a)   By accepting the National Petition for granting
official status to the Welsh language in the courts of
law.
(b)   By establishing a Consultative Committee for
Wales to safeguard Welsh interests during the war,
and to represent the Welsh nation before the
Government.
(c)   By accepting Welsh nationality as sufficient
grounds for conscientious objection to military
service.

A second European war had long been feared, even in the
years before Hitler's rise to power. Constant warnings were
given that the brutal treatment of Germany after the first
world war could create conditions of a German military
resurgence. The unjust clause in the Treaty of Versailles
forcing the German people to admit full guilt for the war
was used by the Allies to justify a villainous reparations
policy, 'squeezing the orange until the pips squeaked' in
Lloyd George's words, which led to the complete collapse
of the German economy. Rampant inflation and a catastrophic slump ravaged the country. I have a boy's
memory of thousands of German marks being sold at a
penny a bundle in Holton Road, Barry. Unemployment
spiralled upwards, poverty was rife and starvation,
inflamed by the callous blockade, was widespread. It
seemed clear the the Weimar Democratic Republic could
not survive unless the Treaty of Versailles were revised. But
there was no revision. German democracy was not given a
chance. The origins of the war lay in the vindictive peace
treaties and the hypocritical decision of the Allies that
Germany must accept all blame and responsibility for caus-

ing the war.

The totalitarian regime which Hitler and the National Socialists imposed in 1933 drastically reduced unemployment and poverty, but it embarked on a hideous persecution of Jews and other non-Aryans, though it was the war itself which made the holocaust possible. Comparatively few Jews were given refuge in Britain. For instance no German Jewish doctors were allowed in; BMA resistance was too strong. The persecution of the Jews was tolerated by many who feared Stalin more than Hitler. It was known that Stalin had eliminated the majority of Communist leaders and had starved millions of Ukrainians to death with two purposes in mind, to enforce collectivisation of farms and to destroy Ukrainian nationalism. These horrors of the 30's were well known to the British public, mainly through splendidly documented books by American journalists and the work of a few English and Welsh journalists. Gareth Jones wrote a series of articles for the *Manchester Guardian* on the horrors he had seen in the Ukraine in 1933 when intellectual acquaintances begged him for a crust of bread and corpses lay untended on the roadside. Roy Medvedev, the Russian historian, calculates the total number of Stalin's victims at about 40 millions. It is not surprising that in the pre-war years many saw little to choose between two loathsome regimes. In any case Anglo British foreign policy is determined not by principle but by English interests, as illustrated by the support given the USA in the Vietnam war.

There had been a lot of discussion among Welsh nationalists about the standpoint they should take when the expected war broke out. The Irish Easter Rebellion led by Patrick Pearse and James Connolly during the first world war, and the actions of Sir Roger Casement were, of course, not unknown. Irish nationalists had traditionally regarded England's extremity as Ireland's opportunity. This was the position of a group of Breton nationalists in the second world war, and it had been Masaryk's position in Austria-Hungary. It was an honourable position, but the stance of Welsh nationalist leaders was different. Although none realised more clearly that war would do nothing to defend Welsh national life, and that Wales had no national freedom to defend, yet nationalists agreed to a policy of Welsh neutrality which rejected support for England's enemies and which made no attempt to weaken England's war effort. Neutrality in the sense of keeping Wales like Ireland out of the war was of course impossible. The Welsh Party's neutrality was designed to concentrate the mind of its members on the defence of the Welsh nation. It necessarily entailed a rejection of England's right to conscript Welsh men and women into the military forces or industry.

Welsh nationalists have two major objectives. The long-term aim is to achieve full national status; the immediate end is to defend and strengthen the nation's life. No other party seeks either objective. In the circumstances of total war, in which all Great Britain's wealth and resources were devoted to defending and strengthening England's life and imperial interests, it was vitally important that some organised body was committed to the defence of Wales, otherwise the total disregard of Welsh values and civilisation, interests and institutions would wreak havoc without check. Churchill proclaimed that the war was fought for survival, although nobody thought for a moment that the life and culture of England were in danger of destruction. The national life and culture of vulnerable little Wales were however in real danger of destruction by assimilation by its huge and powerful neighbour. The danger was illustrated soon after the outbreak of war by Baldwin's declaration to a New York audience: 'We have made one undifferentiated nation of everybody in the island of Britain.' This had been the underlying intent of the 1536 Act of Incorporation and the hope of English governments in the following centuries.

Welsh nationalists were resolved that the nation of Wales would not be terminally dissolved in Baldwin's 'one undifferentiated nation.'

The immediate occasion of Britain's declaration of war was Germany's invasion of Poland, whose system of government was well known to be, in Lloyd George's words, 'the worst feudal system in Europe.' Together with Rumania and Greece, Poland was one of the trio of dictatorships whose integrity was guaranteed by Great Britain. A fourth and more terrible dictatorship became a major ally. Although Britain had a stronger moral case than in 1914, morality had nothing to do with the decision to declare war. As A.J.P.Taylor has said, the war was a struggle for mastery or state survival, 'with Fascism and anti-Fascism thrown in as a top dressing.' Churchill constantly repeated his view that the war was simply for 'Freedom and survival'—for Greater England of course. He fought to achieve unconditional German surrender; Welsh nationalists called for a negotiated peace.

The day it was declared the war's effect on the language and culture of Wales was demonstrated by the abrogation of the few Welsh language radio programmes that hard effort had won. Some time later more hard effort won the restoration of Welsh programmes from 9 to 9.10 a.m. and 7 to 7.10 p.m. The National Eisteddfod almost disappeared. It could be, and was, accommodated in village halls. An early effect on the national party was to reduce the size of its annual conference so much in the first two years that it could meet in the cabin behind the Urdd Gobaith Cymru headquarters in Aberystwyth. Nevertheless party unity and some organisation were maintained in the country.

During the first week of the war a letter appeared in the *Manchester Guardian* and elsewhere over the names of J.E.Daniel, President of the Welsh party, and Saunders Lewis, its former president, appealing for the creation of a non-party movement which could speak to the government on behalf of Wales, its people, language and culture. In consequence a representative conference at Shrewsbury established Pwyllgor Diogelu Diwylliant Cymru (Committee to Safeguard Welsh Culture), later called Undeb Cymru Fydd (New Wales Union), and elected an executive composed of fourteen prominent Welsh people. T.I.Ellis, son of Tom Ellis M.P., was the able secretary, and a network of regional branches was developed. The movement's activities extended from Wales to service men and women abroad and to Welsh men and women conscripted to work in munitions and other industries in England, mainly in the West Midlands. The latter included some 4,000 Welsh women industrial conscripts termed 'surplus unskilled women labour' who were sent to work in England. The Nationalist Party opposed this industrial conscription of Welsh people as vigorously as it opposed military conscription, and supported in tribunals and elsewhere women who refused to go. The Committee to Safeguard Welsh Culture also published a monthly periodical, *Cofion Cymru,* and distributed 26,000 free copies among Welsh people in the armed forces outside Wales.

The first major issue on which the CSWC and the national party cooperated was the seizure by the War Office early in 1940 of 65,000 acres of the hills and valleys of the Epynt Mountain in order to establish an artillery range. This involved evicting a population of hundreds from 60 farms, all Welsh-speaking except half a dozen families on the Brecon side of the mountain. This was therefore the easternmost Welsh-speaking rural community in southern Wales. The community centre was the chapel, Y Babell. It was there the people of Epynt came together to worship, and there their cultural life with its lively eisteddfodau and concerts had its focus. Cwm Cilieni Eisteddfod was the year's biggest social event. One found in Epynt precisely the kind of community that a government concerned for the survival and health of the native language and culture would be most determined to protect. Instead the London government wiped it out.

We fought the outrage as hard as the circumstances of total war allowed. Big audiences filled oil lamp-lit schoolrooms in Merthyr Cynog, Llandeilo'r Fân, Tir Abad, Pentre Felin and Llanfihangel Nant Brân and the halls of Llanwrtyd and Pontsenni. Welsh public opinion was energetically aroused through the press, and the support of public bodies of many kinds was enlisted. J.E.Jones, Plaid Cymru's secretary, visited every one of the 60 farms and confirmed that the local opposition was passionate and unanimous. The families were deep-rooted. The Powells had lived in the same farm for 500 years. Of course the state triumphantly steam-rollered the opposition. The community was eliminated. The families were ejected, their homes becoming artillery targets. Only the foundations of Y Babell remain, and the cemetery. Below, on the banks of the Cilieni, there is now an SAS training point. Blaentalar and Gwybedog, Tafarn Mynydd and Pentre Uchaf have made way for Dixie's Corner and Piccadilly Circus, Gallows Hill and Canada Corner. A populous English military colony was planted nearby, anglicising the villages of Pontsenni, Defynnog and Trecastell, while the anglicising power of the huge range engulfed Llanwrtyd and Llangammarch to the north. The language boundary was pushed ten miles to the west. More land is being added to this vast empty range of heart-breaking beauty. The latest development has been to build at a cost of £5 millions an empty village of 30 houses there, complete with church, shop and pub, to enable the soldiery to pretend they are in Northern Ireland. Epynt epitomises the way our government defends our nation both in war and in peace.

Two of the families ejected from Epynt found farms in Llanddeusant. Within 18 months the two farmers were brought before their betters, as we say in Welsh, in the neighbouring Llangadog court for failing to plough the amount of land required by the wartime regulations. They asked if they could give their evidence in Welsh. Everybody involved in the hearing, including the J.P.'s, clerk and police, was Welsh-speaking. The court granted the request, but the clerk said that the defendants' Welsh must be translated into English, the language of the court. The court's usual interpreter was sent for, Mr.W.J.Gravelle, a former signalman on the line, then Llangadog's leading musician. He duly did his job. The clerk then told the defendants to pay him his fee on their way out. This was a great shock to me. Born and bred in the port of Barry, I had lived in Llangadog for only two years and had no idea that the experience of the two farmers was common in Welsh-speaking Wales. As a trainee solicitor I had seen Arabs and Greeks who had no English coming before the court. They were provided with an interpreter, but of course they did not have to pay for his services. That would have been intolerably unjust. Only Welshmen had to pay to speak their native tongue in a Welsh court of law.

Through The Committee to Safeguard Welsh Culture this case revived the effort which the war had terminated to ensure equality of status for Welsh with English in Wales. A petition to this end had gathered 450,000 signatures in 1938-9 before the war brought the work to an end. The publicity given to the Llangadog case roused a demand for immediate action to implement the petition's policy. The Welsh parliamentary party sent a deputation of five to meet five of us, the first and last time for a body of Welsh M.P.'s to come to Wales to meet representatives of a national movement. The fruit was a feeble Act of Parliament, the Welsh Courts Act, which deleted section 8 of the Act of Incorporation 1536, and permitted a non-English-speaking Welsh person to give evidence in Welsh in a Welsh court of law without having to pay for the privilege. Welsh people who could speak English were still denied the right to give their evidence in Welsh. A few years later I was myself a defendant in the Llangadog court for refusing to pay the radio licence fee during a campaign to restore the Welsh wavelength. When I addressed the court in Welsh, the language of my home and family and the language of the neighbourhood, I was cut down. English was still the only language normally permitted in a Welsh court of law. Consequently Plaid Cymru revived the campaign for equality of status, publishing a pamphlet entitled *Bradychwyd y Ddeiseb* (The Petition has been Betrayed).

The party had fought military conscription before the war. It continued to do so during the war years. Scores of nationalists refused to be conscripted, many on religious as well as nationalist grounds. Of those who stood on nationalist grounds alone fifteen were imprisoned.

The party secured a rare recognition of Wales as a national entity in its successful struggle for an Appeal Tribunal for Wales. It also won the right to conduct cases in the Welsh language. It took four years however to achieve success in its fight for the right of Welshmen in English prisons or in the armed forces to send and receive letters in Welsh, though Poles in the English forces, for example, had always enjoyed the right to send and receive letters in Polish.

The struggle for Welsh language radio programmes persisted throughout the war. After the outbreak of war the only Welsh permitted was five minutes of official announcements from London. Then although the BBC broadcast 5½ hours a day in Spanish to South America and 3¾ hours in Portuguese, for most of the war years Welsh language broadcasts were confined to two ten minute periods a day at poor listening times. The importance of radio broadcasting equalled that of the press as a means of communication during the war.

Under a pre-war plan nearly 200,000 children were evacuated to Wales from London and Liverpool, but the party's pressure for evacuation from the South Wales ports, which were likely to be blitzed, was rebuffed. When the party executive renewed pressure on the Swansea Council as late as 28 December 1940 to organise the evacuation of Swansea children the letter was left on the table. Protest meetings were organised in consequence. A few weeks later the town suffered three nights of appalling bombing.

Nationalist morale was sustained throughout the war among those who read Welsh by Saunders Lewis' 3000 word weekly article in *Y Faner*. In the most brilliant journalism seen in Wales in Welsh or English these articles presented a Welsh standpoint independent of English propaganda. *Y Faner* itself, owned by Kate Roberts and Morris Williams, was a tower of strength to the party, whose two monthly journals, *Y Ddraig Goch* and the *Welsh Nationalist,* were maintained throughout the war, though severely reduced in size. Slowly the party grew. Its growth was reflected in a healthier financial position and in the increasing numbers attending its annual conference and summer school which could be counted in hundreds rather than scores from 1942 on.

When it became clear that Plaid Cymru was not going to fade away it was virulently attacked in 1942 in coordinated articles and pamphlets. Prominent in these scurrilous attacks were Dr.Tom Jones, the Welsh eminence grise and former Deputy Secretary to the Cabinet under three Prime Ministers, and Sir Emrys Evans, principal of Bangor University College. The Reverend Gwilym Davies, a former leader of the Welsh peace movement, was the author of a particularly vicious assault. In two articles Davies contended that the consequence of complete success for Welsh political nationalism would be a fascist, totalitarian, Roman Catholic Wales! Thomas Jones also wrote that the party's narrow and intolerant dogma was inspired by its 'vision of a new promised land of Fascism.' Fascism is a totalitarian creed in which the state swallows the nation. The state is all. 'Everything within the state, nothing outside the state' was Mussolini's slogan. This statism was starkly opposed to Welsh nationalist policies which are decentralist through and through, favouring the widest possible distribution of power. Freedom and Cooperation was our slogan. The Wales we sought to create would be a cooperative commonwealth in which local government would enjoy the maximum possible power. Our nationalism was moderate, democratic and nonviolent, further removed from totalitarian fascism than were the British nationalism and the centralist, militarist, imperialist policies of the Anglo British parties. Yet this absurd accusation of fascism was the kernel of the malicious war-time attacks. The opponents of Welsh nationalism continued to pursue this line for the next three decades. In the later 40's James Griffiths called our young members Hitler Youth, and when I was elected to parliament in 1966 two Welshmen who held high office in Labour governments called me a fascist.

One of the most bitter war-time struggles waged by the party was for the tinplate industry which had been a major industry in the south-west of Wales for half a century. In 1913 Wales produced 822,500 tons of tinplate, the USA 762,583 tons and the rest of the world 91,460. By 1937 the USA had taken the first place but Wales still produced more than the rest of the world. Although the number of men employed had fallen sharply it remained considerable at 28,910. However, the biggest tinplate manufacturer, Richard Thomas Ltd., decided to concentrate its production in a new strip-mill at Redbourne in Eastern England. Under the leadership of Wynne Samuel, whose pamphlet *Save the Welsh Tinplate Areas* presented the case against closure of Welsh tinplate works, Plaid Cymru played a prominent part in the successful opposition. Even Ernest Bevin was moved to speak of manipulation 'by gentlemen sitting in London regardless of its effect on the Welsh nation.' But when the policy of closures was renewed the odds against effective defence of the Welsh-speaking tin-plate communities were as heavy in the circumstances of total war as they had been in the case of the Epynt community. So the closures of the small tinplate works went on apace. 77 were closed by August 1943 and over 14,000 men were uprooted and moved to work in other areas, mainly in England. Within a few years the remainder were closed, and the workers and their families, the majority Welsh-speaking, were forced to leave Wales, never to return, not even when stripmills were opened in Felindre and Trostre. The social and cultural life of the biggest Welsh-speaking industrial area in the south was dealt a savage body blow. Without a government Wales had no chance of defending itself against community destruction.

There was no general election during the war and few by-elections; seats were left uncontested to the party in possession. However when the University of Wales seat became vacant in 1943 the Nationalist Party fought it, with Saunders Lewis as candidate, in the bitterest Welsh by-election for over two decades. Defeating Saunders Lewis was seen, as Hywel Davies has said, as a part of the war effort. The Liberals, who held the seat, took time to find a formidable candidate to carry the establishment banner. W.J.Gruffydd was selected, professor of Welsh in Cardiff University College, an eminent scholar and man of letters who for 20 years had edited *Y Llenor,* the most dis-tinguished Welsh literary journal. Gruffydd had been the acting Vice President of the Nationalist Party when Saunders Lewis was in Wormwood Scrubs. In that office he led the nationalist boycott of George VI's coronation in 1937 which did so much injury to the party. Although Gruffydd won by a substantial majority the status of political nationalism was raised by the vigour of the contest and the force with which Saunders Lewis put the case for the defence of Wales. He also incisively argued the case for a negotiated peace which was urged by Lloyd George and by such distinguished Englishmen as the Bishop of Chichester. Saunders Lewis' case was that if, following a British victory in North Africa, honourable terms were offered to Germany, which had run into deep trouble in Russia, the corps of German generals, who were not without nobility, could accept them and displace Hitler. Churchill and the government bitterly opposed this. Unconditional surrender was their aim. If there had been a negotiated peace many lives would have been saved, including perhaps millions of Jews and gypsies.

Throughout the war, and indeed through the first four decades of its existence, Plaid Cymru fought for the elementary right to have Wales recognised for all purposes as a national entity. In economic matters the final recognition came with the creation of the Welsh Development Authority in 1976. But for Plaid Cymru there would have been no struggle; Wales would have become increasingly an undifferentiated part of England, and parts of Wales would have been united with parts of England for various purposes. That was the will of the British establishment in general and the powerful London bureaucracy in particular. It was reflected in the 1942 Scott Report which urged, not for the first or last time, the creation of development regions in the south and north, in the south by uniting south eastern Wales with the counties on the English side of the Severn, and in the north by union of northern Wales with Cheshire and Lancashire including the Merseyside. Bristol would be the heart of the southern region and Liverpool the centre in the north. The nationalists demanded the balanced development of the whole of Wales with a major north south highway as a part of the programme. No London government has ever attempted this; therefore none has created the infrastructure which would make it possible. Every London government has treated Wales as a peripheral region of England.

It was during the war that the national party began campaigning for what it called a TVA for Wales. The Tennessee Valley Authority was an amazingly successful feature of Roosevelt's New Deal. Based on an intelligent use of electricity it treated the economic, social and cultural life of society as a seamless web. This became the basis of Plaid Cymru's policy in the general election held after the end of the war in Europe.

As the war went on more men from the forces joined the party, and slowly it grew. It became clear that Welsh nationalism was here to stay. Nationalism, which people had been sure would be snuffed out by the war, was stronger at its close than at its start. Scores of people now concentrated their political energies on Wales in contrast to the 'good Welshmen' who gave Welsh national affairs only desultory attention. Despite its diminutive size the party had made quite an impact on the public consciousness. Its major contribution was to keep the idea of Welsh nationhood alive and to awaken a minimum of national political consciousness. But it had also impressed the British establishment with its potential for growth, so much so that at the end of the war Welsh affairs were discussed in Westminster for the first time in nearly half a century in the Welsh Day in Parliament. Further, the Welsh Advisory Reconstruction Council under the chairmanship of Sir J.F.Rees produced a useful report on post-war reconstruction in Wales. Some of the mist which had obscured Wales for decades was being blown away.

In the party's 20 years existence before 1945 the only parliamentary constituency it had fought, apart from the University seat, was Caernarfon, which it contested three times, increasing its vote from 609 in 1929 to 2534 in 1935 in the last general election before the war. It demonstrated its growing strength in 1945 by fighting nine seats, two in by-elections and seven in the general election. The war-time truce between the English parties was still in effect when J.E.Daniel, the party president, obtained 6844 votes, 24.8 per cent, in Caernarfon Boroughs, and Wynne Samuel 6,290, 16.2 per cent, in Neath—the first seat to be contested in the south. In the July general election, after the end of the war in the west but before the war in the east ended, seven seats were contested, gaining 16,017 votes, an average of 2,288 each. Opponents ridiculed the result as derisory, but when compared with the hundreds of votes cast for most Communist or independent candidates it was not insignificant. An independent Welsh political party had made its presence felt electorally for the first time in Welsh history.

This was vital to the survival of the Welsh nation. If there were no political party in which those who had a will to live as a nation were organised, the slide into political oblivion would have continued unchecked. The nation would have died without a struggle. No other political organisation would have fought to ensure a national future. The small nationalist party awakened national conscious-ness in thousands in the political field where the decisions affecting national life are made. In consequence there were tentative signs in London government and parties of a res-toration of a Welsh political dimension after an absence of more than 30 years.

Within weeks of the election, on 6 August, Hiroshima was wiped out by a nuclear bomb. A fortnight later *Y Ddraig Goch,* the party's Welsh-language monthly, carried a leading article which opened with the words, 'With the atomic bomb which destroyed Hiroshima a new era has opened. The power now exists to destroy the human race.' Plaid Cymru has never lost sight of this. Throughout the decades from that time to this it has, alone among the par-ties, unswervingly and unitedly opposed the manufacture, stockpiling and use of nuclear weapons.

5 / The Fight for a Welsh Radio Service

RADIO WAS as powerful a medium of communication as the press from the 20's to the 50's before both the media were overtaken by television. Therefore for three decades a condition of health of the Welsh language and the national life of Wales was an adequate Welsh originated radio service in Welsh and English. Nationalists had no choice but to concentrate on getting a Welsh language service, for when radio broadcasting reached more homes in Wales soon after the establishment of the BBC in 1922 the programmes were wholly English in language and character. Not a minute of Welsh was permitted by the BBC, an arrogantly Anglo British London-centred monopoly whose chairman and eight governors were and still are 'appointed by the Crown', a euphemism for appointment by the Prime Minister of the day. The British Corporation's total exclusion of the Welsh language, then spoken by nearly 40 per cent of the people of Wales, more than twice the present proportion, represented the English establishment's assumption that British was a synonym for English. Contemptuous dismissal of Wales and her national language was in no way incompatible with Britishness.

Five years later, in 1927, there were still no Welsh or English radio programmes broadcast from Wales. The only Welsh heard on the air was a weekly half hour programme broadcast from Dublin by Radio Eireann. This insufferable situation, so typical of the official attitude to Wales in the post-war years, was the first major challenge to be faced by the new little nationalist party. Saunders Lewis took nationalists to the forefront of the struggle, in which Lloyd George was powerfully influential. The struggle for an adequate Welsh radio and then television service was to continue for two generations.

When the nationalists demanded a Welsh-language service the BBC made its reply through E.R.Appleton, director of the Western Region:

> Wales, of its own choice, is a part of the British Commonwealth of Nations, whose official language is English. When His Majesty's Government decided to establish a Corporation for the important task of broadcasting it was natural that the official language should alone be used... To use the ancient languages regularly—Welsh, Irish, Gaelic and Manx—would be either to serve propaganda purposes or to disregard the needs of the greatest number in the interests of those who use the languages for aesthetic and sentimental reasons rather than for practical purposes... If the extremists, who want to force the Welsh language on the listeners of the region, should get their way, the official language would lose its grip.

Appleton's letter encapsulates the contemporary attitude of the Anglo British establishment to Wales. If the position it expresses is unimaginable today who is responsible for the change? Who can deny that but for the nationalists' struggle it is the attitude that would have dominated the last 60 years? Who else has fought for Wales? Of course the attitude still emerges from time to time in occasional outbursts, as in the Rt.Hon.George Brown's angry sexist dictum in Bangor,

> What the little woman spends in the butcher's shop matters more than your bloody language.

But normally Appletonian sentiments are repressed lest more nationalists be created. They have been replaced publicly by plaudits and professions of support for the language which would have horrified the authors of the 1536 Act of Incorporation or the architects of the 1870 Education Act. Demands for the right to use the language

in official and public life are treated with careful respect
even when they are rejected. Appleton's epithet 'extremists'
is still often heard but is applied less to constitutional
nationalists than to those who use direct action.

Pre-war nationalists did more than press for Welsh
language programmes. They demanded a Welsh broadcasting station which would put out programmes in both
Welsh and English. This posited a fundamental change in
the attitude of government to Wales. In the inter-war years
governments regarded Wales as no more than a geographical
expression. A broadcasting station for Wales required her
recognition as a nation. At the time Wales had been incorporated in a Bristol-centred Western Region which included
the whole of south-western England. The BBC insisted that
this region, which coupled Gwynedd and Clwyd with
Gloucester and Somerset and the English south western
counties, had a cultural integrity. It was Arthur's kingdom,
no less! In an article entitled 'The Kingdom of Arthur', the
1934 *BBC Year Book* declared, twelve years after the
Corporation's foundation,

> The West Regional Station re-unites the Kingdom of
> Arthur after years of separation by the Bristol
> Channel.

This comic notion was endorsed by the BBC Controller of
Programmes, a Colonel Dawney, who stated in respose to
nationalist pressure,

> It is felt that the claims of Wales will thus be ade-
> quately met, and I can hold out no hope of any
> reconsideration.

When Ellis Davies M.P. raised the matter in the House of
Commons the press report was brief:

> Mr.Ellis Davies appealed to the Postmaster General
> to establish in Wales a Broadcasting Station in which
> the Welsh language would be used (Loud laughter in
> the House).

Time and again the BBC justified its cultural imperialism

by invoking technical difficulties. When the *BBC Year Book* referred to,

> the demand. . . on nationalist lines for a station devoted to the service of Wales and containing a large proportion of broadcasts in the Welsh language. . .

it declared bluntly,

> The limitation of available wavelengths makes the granting of these minority demands definitely impossible.

The Welsh nationalist response impelled Sir John Reith to declare, 'Welsh nationalists are impervious to reason or fact where broadcasting is concerned'. Fortunately the nationalists were able to rubbish the BBC's contention with the expert advice of a sympathiser, E.G.Bowen, who later took a university chair in Australia, whose knowledge of radio engineering was authoritative. The party mounted a campaign which had the support of most county councils and then of a committee set up by the University Court, which included Saunders Lewis and Lloyd George and which mediated between Wales and the BBC. The obstacle to the BBC's provision of a Welsh service was its refusal to acknowledge the fact of Welsh nationhood. When Melville Dinwiddie was appointed BBC Director for Scotland in October 1934 the *Radio Times* declared that he was 'in charge of the only Broadcasting Region that is also a nation.'

After 13 years of struggle Wales was recognised as an entity in 1935, and in the following year the BBC grudgingly conceded 45 minutes daily of Welsh language programmes, which were increased a little in the next three years. But on the outbreak of war all Welsh-originated programmes were deleted. The struggle began again, but succeeded in getting only two ten minute slots at poor listening times. Obviously justice would not be done to Wales by an imperialist London-centred corporation. Therefore nationalists began their long campaign for an independent Welsh broadcasting corporation. The demand was staunchly supported during the war by Undeb Cymru Fydd (New Wales Union) which organised the meeting which I addressed on the subject during the 1944 Llandybie National Eisteddfod. The address was published as a pamphlet, which sold in thousands, in Welsh and English.

Decades of struggle ensued for an adequate service in both languages. Even in the 50's we were still striving for a minimum and clearly audible service, 30 years after the establishment of the BBC. The Welsh wavelength was taken for service in an English region and replaced by an inferior one which affected the quality of sound adversely and in some areas made the programmes totally inaudible. A Listeners Society (Cymdeithas Gwrandawyr) was formed of some hundreds of nationalists who refused to pay their licence fees and chose to be taken to court to put their case. The original wavelength was restored.

An independent broadcasting corporation continued to be the main objective of incessant campaigning. The support was enlisted of a host of public bodies including local authorities, churches, societies and the university court. Hours of evidence were given to the Beveridge and Pilkington Royal Commissions. Although an independent Welsh corporation has not been achieved the work bore valuable fruit. Without the unremitting campaigning of the nationalists Wales would not have had a measure of federal broadcasting autonomy with a Welsh Broadcasting Council responsible for the BBC's Welsh and English radio and television programmes originating in Wales, nor would the people of Wales be informed, educated and entertained by the splendid service of 12 hours a day in both English and Welsh on Radio Wales and Radio Cymru. This service has made a notable contribution to the unity of Wales and to Welsh national consciousness.

The efforts to keep nationalist persons, nationalist views

and the Nationalist Party off the air are an unhappy chapter in our relations with the medium. They began as early as 1930 when Saunders Lewis was invited to give a talk in English on 'Wales today and tomorrow'. The theme of the script he submitted was the futility of mere cultural nationalism, 'this inoffensive and untroublesome way of being a nation.' It proved too strong for the BBC which rejected it on the grounds that it was 'calculated to inflame nationalist sympathies.'

The English parties have considered it necessary in the post-war years, when Plaid Cymru showed a potential for growth, to keep the party out of news bulletins and to prevent its case being put in political broadcasts. Usually it was the Labour Party which led attempts to censor and silence the nationalists because, as the *Western Mail* reported in November 1953, Labour leaders were alarmed by 'the progress of the Welsh Nationalist movement and the effect upon Socialist policy and membership.' In 1956 however it was Sir David Llewellyn, the Conservative member for Cardiff North, who fired the opening shots. He accused the BBC Welsh news department of a scandalous bias towards Welsh nationalism in comparison with which 'Crichel Down [the great scandal of the day] pales into insignificance.' Labour jumped in on the act. Four Labour M.P.'s supported his call for an inquiry. They were Ness Edwards, a former Postmaster General, James Griffiths, Arthur Pearson and Cledwyn Hughes, a former member of Plaid Cymru. The Conservative Government appointed a committee of inquiry under the chairmanship of Sir Godfrey Ince. The Ince Committee report vindicated the BBC, finding no deliberate or distinct bias. Nevertheless the Corporation was frightened into dismissing the head of the news department and ensuring that less items about Plaid Cymru's activities were broadcast in the future.

For decades Plaid Cymru was denied the right to present its case on the air, although the Beveridge Commission had declared in favour of the right in 1950. Difficulty of communication is still the biggest obstacle in the way of the party's growth. It was in order to mitigate the effect of this that Plaid Cymru for years ran a mobile pirate radio. The situation in the U.K. in the 50's was that a party which fought five per cent of the seats had the right to broadcast. Even in 1945 Plaid Cymru fought 14 per cent of the seats of Wales. In 1954 the Welsh Broadcasting Council decided that four political parties in Wales should be allowed to broadcast for a quarter of an hour annually both in Welsh and English. Plaid Cymru was one of the four. I was called to a meeting of representatives of the parties to be held on 28 January, 1955, to agree to dates. On 20 January however the meeting was cancelled by the BBC following a communication from the unofficial committee of M.P.'s in the House of Commons which distributes the London political broadcasts. The following month three members of the Welsh Broadcasting Council, including Lord Macdonald the chairman, were called before the committee. Lord Macdonald had been a member of the 1945 Labour Government. Clement Attlee and Herbert Morrison were among the Labour M.P.'s present. Morgan Phillips, secretary of the Labour Party, was also there. The committee forbade the Welsh broadcasts under pressure from the Labour members, particularly Herbert Morrison, so Lord Macdonald told me shamefacedly. The deputation reported back to the Broadcasting Council which courageously stood its ground and insisted on its right to put the programmes out. The consequence was a government ban, imposed by Dr.Charles Hill the Postmaster General, the only occasion on which government had imposed a direct veto on broadcasts. Suppression of Plaid Cymru was considered as important as that. *The Times* reported the news under the headline MR.ATTLEE CONCURS. London's fear of Welsh nationalism was deepening. To protest against the ban we held our only rally ever on Trafalgar

Square in conjunction with the SNP and the Commonwealth Party—an English party whose community socialist policies closely resembled ours. We published a book presenting the policies of the three parties under the title *Our Three Nations*. The ban was lifted in 1964 when Plaid Cymru was allowed five minutes each year.

The right to present the party's policies and to be reported in the news bulletins grew enormously in importance with the spread of television. Elections are now media events. As recently as 1964 Plaid Cymru was allowed no time at all on the screen. In the following year the Welsh and Scottish national parties were each granted five minutes a year on radio and television. This was the situation until the 70's. The number of minutes allowed has now been increased to ten annually, confined of course to Wales. They are used as two broadcasts, one in Welsh the other in English. The party therefore still addresses the non Welsh-speaking viewers for five minutes a year only. Far more important than the party broadcasts are the news bulletins, especially those from London. When it is said that elections are fought on the screen it is the London news bulletins that people have in mind. In the 1987 general election the only mention of Plaid Cymru in a London news bulletin was when a joint manifesto with the SNP was published. In the 1989 European election the party was not mentioned at all. Plaid Cymru was literally not in the picture, whereas the English parties are seen and heard, sometimes several times a day on television and radio, during election campaigns and between elections. This is the injustice that does most to impede Plaid Cymru's progess.

6 / In Defence of Land and Community

COMMUNITY HAS a venerable place among Welsh values and the concept is central to nationalist ideology. *Cymdogaeth dda,* literally good neighbourliness, has always been a highly prized quality of Welsh rural and industrial communities, expressed in a warm concern for distressed members of the community. Its prevalence in the mining valleys was an early discovery for me. Then I found it permeated rural Wales too. Soon after I went to live at Llangadog a fire destroyed the small home of a family whose daughter worked for me. Immediately a spontaneous movement in the neighbourhood raised money to rebuild the house. I learnt that people customarily rallied round those struck by illness or who met with a serious accident or a tragic bereavement, giving them substantial help and support. Communal help was the order of the day at harvest time or sheep-shearing. In the Middle Ages communal help was institutionalised in *Cymhortha,* one of the 'sinister usages and customs' which the 1536 Act of Incorporation tried to eliminate. Professor Raymond Williams, whose thinking was so Welsh, wrote of the neighbourliness of his home district of Pandy near Abergavenny as,

> a level of social obligation which was conferred by the fact of seeming to live in the same place and in that sense to have a common identity.

Because community is a basic value for Plaid Cymru nationalists inevitably threw themselves behind the miners when they defended their communities in the 1985 strike.

The concept of community underlies Plaid Cymru's radical

decentralism and cooperative socialism *(cymdeithasiaeth)*. Sharing a common territory is a major factor in creating a sense of community and of common identity, local or national. The Welsh people have shared the land of Wales from time immemorial, and for a thousand years before it was incorporated in England they had a common language, culture, history, law and religion. That is, Wales was a national community, a nation. The depth of the sense of community, local or national, varies largely in relation to size. There are population limits beyond which cities or states cease to have a sense of community among the whole population. But however deep or shallow a sense of community may be it should always be nurtured as an essential element in the quality of personal life. It is in community that a person's full humanity is realised. Fostering community should be a key guideline for civilised government, for its disintegration can transform a neighbourly society into a mass of rootless and footloose beings. Welsh nationalist activities have therefore been directed to defending and strengthening both local communities and the nation, which in nationalist eyes is a community of communities.

The importance nationalists attach to local communities however small has been alien to English establishment thinking. Numbers govern their thought. A significant example of the two different ways of thinking occurred in 1949 when nationalists pressed the Labour government to schedule the quarrying districts of Gwynedd, where unemployment and emigration ravaged the communities, as a development area. Harold Wilson, then Board of Trade minister, refused because the number of unemployed persons was 'not significant in the national total.' The national total was of course that for The United Kingdom of Great Britain and Northern Ireland. A more general example was the 1974 reorganistaion of local government when local council boundaries were based not on community but on the number of inhabitants.

The land of Wales is the homeland of an ancient nation. Its desecration should not be tolerated. Islwyn, last century's greatest Welsh poet, who lived all his life in Sirhywi in Gwent when that district was as Welsh in speech as Llanuwchllyn is today, opens a splendid poem to the land of Wales with the words,

> Everything is sacred, all these mountains
> Have in them heavenly music.

The very different attitude of those who disapprove of fighting for Wales was typified in the aphorism of Iorwerth Thomas, M.P. for Rhondda West, in a radio debate we had in the late 40's. 'Land' he said 'is land'. The concept of a homeland, he said, is 'poetry, just poetry.'

Naturally the defence of Welsh land and the communities it sustains has featured prominently in Plaid Cymru's campaigns, as at Penyberth before the war and Epynt during the war. The defence had to continue with vigour after the war. In answer to a parliamentary question in 1946 Prime Minister Attlee stated that the service departments held 500,940 acres of Welsh land, three times the area held in Scotland. The land taken in Northern Ireland was only seven per cent of the area seized in Wales. A tenth of the total territory of Wales was in the hands of the military service departments. The government found it more agreeable to throw Welsh shepherds out of their heritage than to deny English people of wealth the pleasure of a season's grouse shooting. From Castell Martin and the Preseli in Pembrokeshire to the Hiraethog Mountain and Moel Famau in Clwyd, from the Brecon Beacons and the Carmarthenshire Vans to Cader Idris and Rhobell Fawr, and from the Vale of Glamorgan to Llyn Cerrig Bach in Anglesey (where :.   nest Welsh collection of Celtic artifacts was discovered during the building of the RAF aerodrome) vast tracts of territory had been seized, most of them by far in Welsh-speaking districts. This was another illustration of the government's contemptuous attitude to Wales throughout the quarter of a century after the first world war.

In November 1946 the War Office announced its decision to retain indefinitely 50,000 acres adjacent to the 65,000 acres they occupied in Epynt, in the area of the Carmarthenshire Black Mountains which included Cadair Arthur, Llyn y Fan Fach and Llyn y Fan Fawr. In the depth of winter, January 1947, Plaid Cymru held a protest rally under the great precipice of Cadair Arthur on the shores of Llyn y Fan Fach which attracted wide attention. *Picture Post,* which had a million weekly circulation, made the rally its first feature. The most ambitious project organised by the opposition to the rape of Welsh land were the five resoundingly successful conferences organised by Undeb Cymru Fydd on one Saturday near areas affected. The depth of feeling in Maenclochog, where people stood two-deep round the hall and sat on the window sills, remains etched on the mind. Did not the War office intend turning the whole of Preseli, an area of exceptionally rich culture, into an Epynt-like gunnery range? Were not 105 of the 204 farms on the mountain to be wholly requisitioned and parts of the land of the other 99 to be taken? Was not half the village of Mynachlog Ddu, where Waldo Williams learnt his Welsh, within the range including the school where Waldo's father was headmaster? In 1930, when four-fifths of the people of Mynachlog Ddu attended Bethel Baptist chapel, 99 per cent of the population was Welsh-speaking. (Today, after two decades of in-migration only two Welsh-speaking families remain in the village). Nearly half Bethel's members would lose their homes to the range and a further 79 would be badly affected. The two leaders of the local opposition were Joseph James, a minister with the Welsh Independents who came from Dowlais, and Parri Roberts, a Baptist minister from Anglesey, both colourful characters. Both planned to move to cottages on the range when the artillery was in place. Their patriotism fused with anti-militarism, a common combination, which added fuel to their fire. Preseli was saved.

When the War Office announced its intention of adding ten thousand acres in the Abergeirw district to its territory adjoining the Trawsfynydd military camp, Plaid Cymru again mounted an opposition movement with strong support from the cultured Abergeirw community. After a lively rally which showed the strength of local and national feeling the most dramatic incidents were at the camp itself. For two days the camp was contained by a phalanx of road sitters who closed the roads to the west and the east, preventing vehicles from entering or leaving. These events inspired Bertrand Russell and Michael Scott to form the anti-nuclear Committee of a 100. The army was helpless in face of this nonviolent siege. A couple of angry officers urged lorry drivers to push their lorries against our backs but no more. One lorry driver leaned out of his cab and told me, 'You're alright mate.' The camp commandant was in constant touch with his Shrewsbury headquarters, but use of violence would have been a moral defeat. Nor could the police use violence without loss of public sympathy. Our command of the situation was shown by an incident when I was standing with the camp commandant and the chief constable of Gwynedd. A soldier came up to the commandant, saluted and asked if he could bring his lorry through, 'Don't ask me, ask him', said the commandant referring to the chief constable. The soldier went to the chief constable, saluted and made the same request. 'Don't ask me, ask him', said the chief constable, referring him to me. He turned to me, saluted and repeated the request. 'What are you carrying?', I asked. 'Food', he said. 'That's alright', I said, 'Tell them you have permission to bring it through.' 'But they won't believe me. I'll have to have a pass', he said. So I wrote a note in Welsh. He looked at it and exclaimed, 'Gor blimey, bloody Russian.'

In consequence of the opposition a public inquiry, in which nationalists put their case against the land seizure, was held in Dolgellau under the chairmanship of Sir Wyn Wheldon. It found against the War Office. The Abergeirw community remained intact. This angered Iorwerth Thomas M.P. Those who had contained the camp were, he said, 'madmen whose foolish actions would lead to the shedding of blood and civil war.'

The idea that the land of Wales was up for grabs spread to other government agencies. In 1950 the Forestry Commission published an outrageous plan to plant one and a quarter million acres of Welsh land: another brazen example of the establishment's attitude to Wales. Once again Plaid Cymru campaigned to expose its consequences and to rouse local and national opposition. As an example of the Forestry Commission's destruction of an old cultured pastoral community the Party publicised the effect of the vast Cothi forest where thousands of acres of cereal growing land as well as fine pasture land had been planted. Scattered through the forest were ruined homes and farmsteads where families had been bred which had enriched the life of the local and national community. Gwenallt, the great Glamorgan poet, sang in his poem *Rhydcymerau* of the fate of the community, of which some of his own forbears were members.

> And by this time there's nothing there but trees.
> Impertinent roots suck dry the old soil:
> Trees where neighbourhood was,
> And a forest that once was farmland.
> Where was verse-writing and scripture
>   is the South's bastardised English.
> The fox barks where once cried lambs and children,
> And there, in the dark midst,
> Is the den of the English minotaur;
> And on the trees, as if on crosses,
> The bones of poets, deacons, ministers, and teachers
>   of Sunday School
> Bleach in the sun,

And the rain washes them, and winds lick them dry.
(Tony Conran's translation)

The first step in the Forestry Commission's monstrous plan
was to be the compulsory purchase, with the assent of the
Minister of Agriculture, of tens of thousands of acres in the
upper Tywi Valley. If this land were seized without opposition the Commission could proceed confidently with the
whole of its grandiose project. Plaid Cymru alone was sufficiently concerned to defend the pastoral community living
in the threatened hills. Our campaign in public meetings
and the press won the support of many public bodies,
including local authorities. A thousand people attended a
colourful rally held in a spectacular location above a pre-
cipitous 300 foot drop to the juncture of the Doethie
torrent and the Tywi river and facing Twm Siôn Catti's
cave in the steep wooded mountainside. Sir Rhys Hopkin
Morris M.P., whose presence surprised us, was invited to speak.
Once again the opposition compelled the government to
hold a public inquiry, at which Hopkin Morris distinguished himself, and once again the inquiry found in
favour of the case for the defence. Henceforth the Forestry
Commission had to move with more circumspection. Land
could not be seized on a huge scale nor communities
destroyed.

In 1950 the Electricity Board, another government
agency, announced a hideous hydro-electric scheme in
Gwynedd which would have ravaged some of the most
enchantingly beautiful countryside in Wales and caused
widespread agricultural injury. The scheme involved the
construction of 80 miles of tunnelling, 40 miles of open
ditches, 17 fire stations, 23 reservoirs, 22 dams and 4½
miles of uncovered pipes and concrete canals in Eryri. In
those pre-green days when the English parties gave no
thought to the environment the main burden of the defence
fell on Plaid Cymru's shoulders, though in this matter it
had the full support of the Council for the Preservation of

Rural Wales. The pinnacle of the opposition campaign was the rally attended by 1,500 people organised with the CPRW's cooperation in the breath-taking beauty of Nant Gwynant. The chair was taken by Mr.W.R.P.George, then Vice President of Plaid Cymru, and Lady Megan Lloyd George was among the speakers. Once again the opposition was successful; the Electricity Boards plans were withdrawn.

Although nationalists opposed the plan to drown Cwm Clywedog in vain, the opposition to building a huge reservoir in Cwm Dulais was successful. The intended reservoir would have destroyed one of the few Welsh-speaking communities left in Breconshire.

These campaigns raised the nationalist profile. In August 1950 Goronwy Roberts M.P. (later Lord) wrote in alarm.

> 'The Nationalist Party is growing. . . Many of our own people are dispirited and frustrated. They find it difficult to counter the arguments of the separatists. The facts are so positive. Have we got a Welsh policy? Unless we change our attitude, we shall reap an inevitable whirlwind. There are disquieting signs of this already.'

The fight for local territory and communities is related to the party's long struggle for the territorial and national integrity of Wales. The major issue it fought was the status of Monmouthshire, now Gwent. The county had been separated from the other twelve counties of Wales and placed in the Oxford circuit. Its relation to the rest of Wales was not dissimilar to the relation of the Six Counties to the rest of Ireland. The phrase used since 1536 was Wales and Monmouthshire. Yet there was no doubt about the Welsh character of Monmouthshire. Iolo Morganwg had asserted at the beginning of the 19th century that the county had a bigger proportion of monoglot Welsh-speaking people than any other in Wales. The vast majority of the Chartists who rose in 1839 were Welsh-speaking. Under the leadership of D.J. and Noelle Davies nationalists fought the issue for decades against the Monmouthshire is English Society led by Lord Raglan, Sir Mathers Jackson and Newport's town clerk. Numerous meetings were held, press articles and letters written and local and parliamentary elections fought in the county. Two 30 page pamphlets by D.J.Davies and Dafydd Jenkins were published. Pamphleteering was then an effective means of propaganda. Thousands of copies of each were sold.

The Welsh status of Monmouthsire was finally secured in consequence of the 1966 nationalist victory in Carmarthen. The Beeching Commission had long been considering the matter of legal administration in England and Wales. Dewi Watkin Powell wrote a memorandum on the position of Wales which we presented in the Commission's office. Fortunately the secretary, an Irishman, was sympathetic, but he had to tell us that the Welsh section of the Commission's report had been completed. Wales was to be divided. Southern Wales was to be administered from Bristol and northern Wales from Liverpool. Nevertheless in view of our Carmarthen success the Commission was persuaded to reconsider the matter in the light of our memorandum. On my third visit to the office I was told that our proposals had been accepted, 'reluctantly' said the published report. The country would be adminstered as an entity from Cardiff, and for the first time since 1536 Monmouthshire would be acknowledged to be an integral part of Wales. Before long the county's name was changed to Gwent, and the old phrase Wales and Monmouthshire was heard no more.

As early as 1935 the party conference had called for the recognition of Cardiff as the Welsh capital city, and during the next two decades the party constantly pressed for its official acknowledgement. Substantial support was given by local authorities and other public bodies despite the case presented by such other towns as Machynlleth and Caernarfon. Of a statement we published in 1955 a *Western Mail* leading article said that to try to improve on it would be 'gilding the lily'. In 1956 the day was won. The government recognised Cardiff as the capital city of Wales, and during the next two decades Cardiff on several occasions gave leadership which only a capital city can give. Although it will only be nominally a capital until it becomes the seat of parliament and government yet its recognition helped to reinforce the sense of national integrity just as the recognition of Monmouthsire as a part of Wales was to do later.

Defence of the land of Wales was more often than not inseparable from the defence of community, as in Epynt and Tryweryn. But communities can be threatened, as the striking miners of 1985 were aware, by removing the prime means of livelihood. Such was the situation in Cwmllynfell where the men of the village were almost all dependent on the local coalmine. Cwmllynfell was a Welsh-speaking community on the eastern end of the anthracite coalfield. Few now remember how rich the culture of the anthracite coalfield was. Its cultural wealth was strikingly illustrated in the experience of Dr.Gomer Roberts, the erudite historian of Welsh Methodism. He had been working for years in the Pencae pit in Llandybie when he decided to try to take a university degree. He was helped to go to college by six miners in that part of the anthracite coalfield. One of them was Amanwy, James Griffiths' brother. The six were poets. They cooperated in publishing a book of their own poetry, *O Lwch y Lofa* (From the Dust of the Mine), sold it widely and gave Gomer Roberts the profit to help him on his way. Where but in Wales could that happen? It was his knowledge of this popular intellectual Welsh culture that impelled H.N.Brailsford, the great socialist, to say after a debate in the Neath Gwyn Hall on the nationalisation of the coalmines versus cooperative ownership and control, that the latter would be practicable in Wales though not in England, 'because your people have culture'.

The Cwmllynfell pit produced the best red vein anthracite coal. When the decision to close it was anounced in 1962 representatives of Plaid Cymru held two meetings with the colliery lodge, whose chairman Isaac Stephens was a nationalist, and one with the 300 miners. The colliers accepted the Plaid Cymru plan for running the mine as a cooperative. The party's policy of industrial cooperative democracy, which was spelt out most fully by the Machynlleth conference the year after the Cwmllynfell closure, was far closer to Noah Ablett's *Miners' Next Step* than to Labour's policy of state nationalisation. The Plaid Cwmllynfell plan was devised in detail by Wynne Samuel, who also found a market in Holland for the coal. The miners would have not only kept their jobs but would have gained financially. But all the powers that be were united in opposition, not only the Conservative government and the NCB but also the NUM and the Labour Party, which could not tolerate a variation on its nostrum of centralised nationalisation. James Griffiths declared that if the Cwmllynfell mine were run on cooperative lines that would be the end of nationalisation. The miners decided to stage a stay-in strike, but when the NCB told them they would have to nominate another pit of the same size for closure their resistance collapsed.

The bitter hostility of the Labour establishment to the cooperative control of a coalmine indicated the length they would go in defence of state nationalisation. Even more significant in this respect was the antagonism of the Labour group which controlled the Carmarthenshire County Council to a motion in my name and that of my namesake, Gwynfor S.Evans of Betws, on the question of pneumoconiosis. More suffered from this terrible disease, which hardened lungs like concrete, in the Carmarthenshire anthracite coalfield than anywhere else. In every anthracite coalfield village the emaciated frames of men with racking coughs, struggling for breath, were an everyday sight. In the last stages of the disease many were bedridden with oxygen cylinders at the bedside. The Medical Research Council which investigated one big colliery found that the lungs of only 28 per cent of the men worked normally after working between ten and twenty years. Plaid Cymru had always had a deep concern about the situation. Although the disease was avoidable, next to no effective steps were taken to prevent it, and when it was contracted the treatment of the men was abominable. The NCB would do everything possible to avoid paying compensation. It was generally said that a silicotic miner had to have one leg in the grave before he was considered to deserve any compensation at all. And when men died of pneumoconiosis few widows received compensation. The cause of death on the death certificate would usually be heart failure, pneumonia, tuberculosis, anything but pneumoconiosis. Plaid Cymru published a powerful pamphlet in the forties exposing the situation by D.J.Davies, who had himself been a miner in the anthracite coalfield.

For six months a group was convened in Ammanford by Dr.D.H.Davies to study the position. It included men who had long experience of every aspect of the problem, underground and above ground, medical, insurance, historical and practical. The minutes of the NUM and the SWMF over scores of years were examined to discover the response of the unions. The fruit was a ten-point policy which filled three pages of the agenda of the next county council meeting. In those days the council was the county health authority. When I rose to propose the motion the leader of the Labour group jumped to his feet to demand that the motion be ruled out of order. The chairman who was a part of the plot of course agreed that it was unconstitutional. I protested that it was ridiculous to maintain that the county health authority was not concerned with the health of miners in the county. And had not the council discussed in recent years such matters as nuclear weapons and the Suez War which were certainly not within the purview of its authority or related to it? As I persisted in arguing against the chairman's grotesque ruling my voice was drowned in uproar from the Labour benches, to which my seconder, now on his feet with me added his passionate voice—his father had died of pneumoconiosis. The chairman shouted that the meeting was closed and left the chair. The reason for Labour determination that the council should not discuss a disease which ravaged the county's mining community as nowhere else, was that prevention and adequate compensation would place too heavy a financial burden on a nationalised industry.

A similar situation existed in the quarrying industry. When a minority Labour government in 1978 needed the support of the three Plaid Cymru M.P.'s, Dafydd Wigley and Dafydd Elis Thomas made justice to the widows of silicotic quarrymen one of the conditions of our continued support.

Despite the constant closure of Welsh coalmines the NCB and NUM succeeded, in cooperation with the local authorities, in transferring Durham miners and their families to the Welsh-speaking Gwendraeth area of the anthracite coalfield in order to relieve unemployment in north-east England. Plaid Cymru alone opposed this foolish policy, later regretted, which was an obvious blow to the community and cultural life of the Gwendraeth. The opposition was led by Emrys Roberts, who organised and spoke at a series of public meetings.

The coal and quarrying industries were doomed to decimation. Under the first post-war Labour government mines were closed on an increasing scale. The process continued under the 13 years of Conservative government but reached its peak when Labour returned to power in 1964. During the six years of Labour government 1964-70 a Welsh mine was closed every 6½ weeks on average. There were 60,000 fewer people in employment in Wales in 1970 than when Labour came to power in 1964 and unemployment doubled in that period.

The Cwmllynfell episode was the only chance Plaid Cymru had of applying its cooperative policy to heavy industry, but its members often set up cooperatives including three in Merioneth, the creamery at Rhydymain, a woollen factory at Dinas Mawddwy and a printing works and local paper at Dolgellau. In Glamorgan, Plaid established cooperatives at Mountain Ash and Merthyr Tydfil.

All the party's efforts to create work and to oppose industrial closures were made with the defence of community in mind. This was even more obvious in its opposition to the overspill plans of the early 60's. When Liverpool was bursting at the seams and rural Wales was being steadily depopulated it was proposed that the pressure on Liverpool be relieved and parts of rural Wales repopulated by transferring people from the English city to the Welsh countryside. As part of this absurd plan ten thousand people would be moved, hopefully with accompanying industry, to Llangefni in Ynys Môn, and another ten thousand to Bala in Merioneth. Neither Llangefni nor Bala had a population of 2,000. T.W.Jones, later Lord Maelor, the Labour M.P. for Merioneth, was enthusiastic about this inundation which he said would bring so much work and wealth to Penllyn. Nationalists threw their weight against it and mobilised the opposition. Nothing came of it.

The depopulation of mid-Wales attracted much attention in those years. The remedy was balanced development which demanded an adequate infrastructure, including a north-south highway, but it was never adopted. The unbalanced idea produced by Jim Griffiths and fervently propagated when he was appointed first Secretary of State for Wales in 1964, was to build a town of 60,000 people at Newtown in the Severn valley. Most of the new citizens to repopulate this part of mid-Wales would have come from Birmingham and the English Midlands, creating a Brumon-Severn twice the size of Shrewsbury. The remedy was worse than the disease. Again the opposition succeeded in aborting the plan.

These problems were diminutive in comparison with the massive in-migration, almost wholly from England, in the 70's and 80's. Close on a million people moved into Wales during those two decades. At the end of the 80's they were streaming in at the rate of three quarters of a million in ten years. A decade's influx would amount to over 27 per cent of the population of Wales, the equivalent of twelve million immigrants into England. In comparison the number which may enter from Hong Kong is insignificant.

These immigrants caused grave housing and other problems in every part of the country without exception. The character of hundreds of small communities has been changed, scores have been destroyed. Most dangerously the enormous extent of the immigration threatens to denude Wales of communities where Welsh-speaking people are a majority. Since the survival of the language depends on the existence of Welsh-speaking communities, and since the long-term survival of a national sense of identity depends on the survival of Welsh as a community language, the mass immigration threatens the existence of Welsh nationhood. The crisis will be discussed in the chapter on the language.

The only countries which have suffered mass immigration on the Welsh scale are Estonia, where 40 per cent of the country's 1½ million population are immigrants, mainly Russian, and Latvia where 50 per cent of the 2½ million people are immigrants, also mainly Russian. In these countries mass immigration has been the chief factor giving nationalism its irreversible momentum. Latvians and Estonians felt their nations were being destroyed. Yet neither country is as vulnerable as Wales. The loyalty of Latvians and Estonians to their small nations is rock solid. Both had parliaments, which gave them an immense advantage over Wales. Two years ago citizenship laws were passed to control immigration. Their peaceful nationalist movements will soon have achieved full self-government in both countries. Together with Lithuania, they have initiated the decomposition of the Russian Empire and the democratising of many Soviet republics on the basis of nationhood, just as Plaid Cymru aims to create a Welsh democracy on the basis of Welsh nationhood. The strength of their nationalist parties will ensure the survival of these remarkable Baltic nations. A national future for Wales will be secured only when the Welsh people give comparable support to their nationalist party.

7 / Tryweryn

THE FIGHT for Cwm Tryweryn's land and community resounded in industrial as well as in rural Wales. Echoes of the campaign are still heard; some of its consequences still remain. A remarkable consequence came to light when Cabinet papers for the end of the 50's were released in 1989 under the 30 years rule. They revealed that it was fear of nationalist resurgence after the drowning of Cwm Tryweryn that impelled the Conservative government to locate the huge stripmill at Llanwern rather than Grangemouth in Scotland where there was high unemployment at that time. In a memorandum to the Cabinet, Heathcote Amery, Chancellor of the Exchequer, warned of the political consequences of siting the stripmill, which would employ 7,000 men, outside Wales.

> There is still resentment in Wales over the support given by the Government to Liverpool's Bill for flooding part of the Tryweryn Valley in Merioneth... If the Government were now to stop the building of the stripmill in Wales, criticism of the Government would be greatly intensified and Welsh nationalist feeling aroused. The dangers of such a situation must not be underrated.

Henry Brooke, then Minister for Welsh Affairs, strongly supported the Chancellor. No one was more aware of the Welsh situation than Brooke. Had he not been humiliated by the Eisteddfod Council's cancellation of the address he was to have given from the platform of the Llangefni National Eisteddfod because of the deep public anger aroused by his support for Liverpool's plan to drown Cwm

Tryweryn?

Although the Tryweryn campaign was lost it is a striking example of the establishment's fear of Welsh nationalism. Nationalism is the only political force in Wales respected and feared by the London establishment. Though the national party may be small it is London's estimate of its potential which counts. After all, nationalism is the greatest moral power in the world, as the British, Russian, American, French and other empires learnt to their cost. Locating the stripmill in Llanwern is an instance of the length to which the government will go to hold it back. Nationalism is the one strong weapon the Welsh people have in their fight for freedom and justice. Small though Plaid Cymru was, its nationalism had radically changed the political debate in Wales for every party. If Scottish nationalism had been as strong and vigorous as Welsh nationalism the stripmill decision could have been different, but in the 1959 election the SNP fought only 5 of the 71 Scottish seats, whereas Plaid Cymru fought 20 of the 36 in Wales.

The culture and tradition of the community in Cwm Tryweryn retained its strength and integrity to the day of its dissolution. Drowning the valley and the little village of Capel Celyn was the clearest exposure in our time of Welsh political servitude. Although far more land was appropriated and more families dispersed when the War Office destroyed the Epynt community in 1940, war-time circumstances severely restricted the defence. Whereas Epynt was autocratically seized by a government department, Cwm Tryweryn was drowned by Liverpool Corporation in the teeth of strong national resistance after a hearing in the House of Lords and a debate in the House of Commons. One Welsh M.P. alone voted for the Liverpool parliamentary Bill, but Welsh opposition was swept aside by a huge majority of English M.P.'s. The Westminster Parliament, the only parliament Wales has, was exposed as an English Parliament in which English interests are supreme.

Penllyn, in which Cwm Tryweryn is found, is a district of five parishes known throughout Wales for the quality of its popular intellectual culture, comparable with Llŷn, which was struck by the Air Ministry in 1936. The first the people heard of the threat to their homes was in a *Liverpool Daily Post* report in December 1955. In the absence of any warning the shock was severe. The corporation of a city whose wealth and population exceeded that of northern Wales felt that to consult the people they intended evicting was superfluous. Nor was any local authority consulted or informed, parish, district or county. Had not Liverpool destroyed a Welsh-speaking community with impunity earlier in the century at Llanwddyn in order to create Lake Vyrnwy to supply the city and Cheshire conurbations with water? Did not Birmingham destroy a Welsh-speaking community at Claerwen to build the Elan Valley reservoirs? And had not the Alwen and Brenig reservoirs been built without bother to serve Birkenhead and Bootle? Seizure of Welsh land and resources had been common practice. But when the Vyrnwy, Elan and other huge reservoirs were built Wales was defenceless. She had no national party to fight for her. Liverpool thought, as the London government had found in the inter-war decades, that Welsh interests could be ignored with impunity.

For some time Liverpool water officials had been prowling round the Welsh countryside in search of a site. Eventually they made a pretence of settling on a valley in Montgomeryshire at Llanfihangel-yng-Ngwynfa. The city's intention of making a reservoir there was declared. This district was venerated by all who cared about Welsh life and literature. It was there in Dolanog that Ann Griffiths had lived all her short life, a saint whose hymns give her a central place in European Christian poetry. As Liverpool officials had calculated, the Welsh public was outraged.

There was a tremendous outcry throughout the land and Liverpool magnanimously withdrew. Of course it had never intended making a reservoir there. Dolanog was a decoy to draw Welsh fire. An engineers' report, prepared before the Tryweryn decision was brought to light in the later House of Lords hearing. It stated,

> Serious consideration has been given to the Dolanog Dam site on the River Vyrnwy. However, the gross yield from this source is some 20 million gallons a day, which would not go very far to solving Liverpool's problems.

They estimated the cost to be £2,500,000 more than the Tryweryn scheme, which would give double the yield of water. 'We consider the Tryweryn scheme to be the most economical solution', said the report. Nevertheless Liverpool proclaimed its intention of drowning Dolanog and deeply impressed the Welsh people when, with a great show of magnanimity, it bowed to the outraged opinion of the Welsh, and withdrew the scheme.

Plaid Cymru had suspected a cynical ploy, and declared in its annual rally on September 19 that it would oppose Liverpool aggression wherever it occurred. This angered Alderman Cain, Chairman of the Liverpool Water Committee, who contrasted 'intolerant nationalists' with 'those whose obvious dignity and patience and sincerity (over Dolanog) were bound to make an impression on the Liverpool City Council.'

As Plaid Cymru's parliamentary candidate in Merioneth since 1945 I had come to know Penllyn and Cwm Tryweryn well, and had learnt to admire its cultural wealth. In the evening entertainments of the *noson lawen,* often held in large farmhouse kitchens, I was astonished by the quality of contributions by individuals and groups. They excelled in *penillion* singing, an ancient mode in which poems are sung to an original counterpoint woven around a harp melody. Penllyn boasted of twenty or more harpists.

Poets abounded. Elwyn Edwards, a poet born in Capel Celyn, now under the water, won the chair in the 1988 Newport National Eisteddfod. A competition which always amazed me was the recitation of the biggest number of *englynion*. An *englyn* is a four-line epigramatic verse composed in *cynghanedd,* a complicated system of rhymes and chiming consonants. Competitors were not allowed to repeat an *englyn* already heard or to recite more than one of a *cadwyn* (chain) of *englynion.* The competition could last for an hour, such was the remarkable store of verses in the memory of the people assembled, mainly farmers and their wives and children.

Elizabeth Watcyn Jones, the secretary of the Tryweryn Defence Committee, was one of these people. Her father, Watcyn o Feirion, who kept the Capel Celyn post office, now at the bottom of Llyn Celyn, was a well-known poet and musician and a master of the art of *penillion* singing. He conducted a popular male voice choir in which one of the tenors was Bob Tai'r Felin, renowned in Wales as a folk singer. The star of many a *noson lawen* Bob struck his top G like a bell when in his eighties. Watcyn o Feirion's younger daughter was seven times a National Eisteddfod winner. In a 280 page book, *Cofio Tryweryn,* his son Watcyn has recounted the history of Tryweryn and the fight against the submergence of the valley, the latter based largely on the minutes kept by his sister Elizabeth, who herself published a book on Poland, *Teithio Pwyl,* which is a fascinating introduction to the life history and culture of that troubled land, her husband's homeland. In a letter to the *Liverpool Daily Post* at the time of the struggle, Gertrude Armfield wrote,

> The way of life nurtured in these small villages which serve, with their chapel and school as focal points, a wider population—this way of life has a quality almost entirely lost in England and almost unique in the world. It is one where a love of poetry and song, the spoken and written word, still exists, and where

recreation has not to be sought after and paid for, but is organised locally in home, chapel and school.

This was the nature of the Tryweryn community, whose chapel and school, like the post office and shop, would soon be engulfed by an enormous reservoir.

The community vigorously opposed this fate. Staunch and united, it was as resolute at the end of the long campaign as in the beginning, despite the financial temptation of big compensation money. 'You can talk of compensation', said Councillor David Roberts, Caefadog, chairman of the Defence Committee, after the second reading of Liverpool's parliamentary Bill, 'it is not compensation we call for, but to keep our homes.'

The Tryweryn Defence Committee was formed immediately after the news of Liverpool's intention broke, with two valley people as secretary and chairman, Elizabeth Watcyn Jones and David Roberts. My own association with the committee was due to my candidature in, Merioneth. T.W.Jones, Labour M.P. for Merioneth, put in an appearance only when the campaign was well advanced. One of its first actions, after a packed protest meeting in Bala, was to ask the Liverpool City Council to receive a deputation including Sir David Hughes Parry, Sir Ifan ap Owen Edwards and other national figures. This was brusquely refused, as was a later request, on the grounds that the council's policy was never to receive deputations. Before the end of the campaign this was discovered to be untrue. The attitude adopted by the Labour-controlled council was arrogant from the outset, most typically expressed by Alderman John Braddock and his wife Bessie Braddock M.P.

The image painted by the council of its Welsh opponents was of people lacking ordinary humanity who would deny the wretched people of Liverpool even a cup of clean water. This was also the picture painted by Henry Brooke, the Minister for Welsh Affairs, who acted throughout the struggle as Minister for Liverpool Affairs. He predicted that water shortages might occur in the next few years on Merseyside and in South West Lancashire, adding,

> I cannot believe that the preservation of the Welsh way of life requires us to go as far as that. I cannot believe that the Welsh people of all people want to stand outside the brotherhood of man to that extent.

We responded by adapting Chesterton's words to a famous Liverpudlian, Chuck it, Brooke. For the people of Liverpool were in fact already getting more than enough water from Wales at the cheapest price in Britain, not only for drinking and washing but for baths, toilets, watering gardens, washing cars and for industry. Much of the water they took without payment was sold to neighbouring conurbations at a big profit. Tryweryn water was to be taken to meet not the personal needs of individual people but of anticipated new industry and for profitable sale. Subsequently it became clear that even the new industrial needs were greatly exaggerated and might have been met from existing Welsh sources. Examination of the city's Water Committee books for the 35 years between 1920 and 1955 showed that consumption of water had increased by only 4.4 million gallons a day. Liverpool was already taking 50 m.g.d. from Lake Vyrnwy, and it had the right to abstract 10 m.g.d. from the Dee. In addition Birkenhead and Bootle were taking huge amounts from lakes Alwen and Brenig. Such information as this was obtained through the labours of Dr.Dafydd Alun Jones, then a medical student, who in the week before his final exams spent three days and nights going through the books of the Liverpool Water Committee from 1860 on.

If the need for new sources of industrial water was as urgent as Liverpool maintained, we contended that it should be obtained from such English sources as the Lake District. But this, said the city authorities, would raise the price of the water and make industrial competition more difficult. Profit, not necessity, was the nub. Henry Brooke underlined this in saying that Wales was 'the most obvious and the cheapest source of water for Liverpool.'

The Welsh case was set forth in a 26-page pamphlet and pressed home in public meetings, articles, letters, resolutions by local councils and various other public bodies, including trade unions such as the NUM. Of the 1,055 bodies which protested 125 were local authorities. This aspect of the campaign was organised by J.E.Jones, Plaid Cymru's general secretary, from the party's central office. Branches of Plaid Cymru in England were also active. Welsh societies in England were addressed by Watcyn Jones and others. The Liverpool Welsh had their own defence committee which organised a big protest meeting in the city. Meetings were held in Birmingham and London, where the defence committee was particularly active. A rally organised by Plaid Cymru on the banks of the Tryweryn on 29 September, 1955, was attended by 1,500 people. The assistance of the Merioneth County Council was to prove particularly helpful, and Penllyn District Council gave staunch support throughout the campaign. Of the Welsh local authorities only fifteen refused to notify Liverpool of their opposition. The supportive councils included such Labour authorities as the Rhondda, Pontypridd, Abercarn, Ebbw Vale, Brynmawr and Mynydd Islwyn. Even Chepstow on the extreme south-eastern border backed the opposition. Editorial support was given by the *Western Mail* and all the Welsh-language press without exception.

The people of Cwm Tryweryn itself threw themselves energetically into the struggle. On 21 November 1956 every one of the inhabitants of the threatened part of the valley marched in protest, with placards and banners flying, through the centre of Liverpool, a most courageous communal act unique in Welsh annals. What huge city in England had ever seen a small mountain community, men, women and children, demonstrating in its heart? This was followed on another occasion by a journey to Manchester to make a live programme on the new medium of television.

Because the Liverpool City Council had refused to receive a deputation from Wales, Mr.David Roberts, Caefadog, Dr.Tudur Jones, principal of Bala-Bangor College, and I decided to try to make our voice heard in the council. Through the kindness of Councillor Lawrence Murphy, an Irishman with nationalist leanings who was a friend of Dr.Dafydd Alun Jones, we obtained a copy of the agenda to note when the Tryweryn issue would rise. There was no public gallery above the council chamber. We sat in the front row of public seats behind the back row of councillors. Immediately in front of me was the solid figure of Mrs.Bessie Braddock. When the Tryweryn matter was reached I got up and addressed the chair. No sooner had I started to speak than Mrs.Braddock shouted at the top of her voice and banged the lid of her desk up and down. Most other councillors seemed to follow her lead as I continued to try to speak. My voice and that of the chairman were lost in the uproar which continued until the police were called in to take us out. This did the council no good, for a month later I was given the rare if not unprecedented privilege of addressing the council for a quarter of an hour.

We discovered sympathy among some non-Labour members. When the adoption of Liverpool's parliamentary Bill was put to the vote a number abstained in order to indicate their disapproval. Aldermen Braddock and Cain had sufficient reason for their absence on that day. They were in Westminster. The *Liverpool Daily Post* reported that they were in the House of Commons with Liverpool's chief water engineer, 'to discuss the passage of the Bill through Parliament with the Welsh Socialist members.' From the outset the Welsh Labour M.P.'s had been in collusion with Liverpool's Labour M.P.'s. Even the member for Merioneth gave the defence no support in the early stages. He failed to turn up to the first public protest meeting in Bala and absented himself from the early meetings of the Defence Committee. It was only after the opposition gathered strength that he made a show of support. His brother, Idwal Jones, Labour M.P. for Wrexham, justified him on the ground that the opposition was a Plaid Cymru stunt. He declared,

> We owe Plaid Cymru no obligation to affirm or deny anything. They do not represent Wales, neither in numbers nor, I am pleased to think, in outlook. Wales should beware of this anti-gwerin movement steeped so deeply in the cult of the leader: it is anti-England, and in the final resort anti-Welsh.

The seizure of Welsh land and resources and the destruction of community seemed as acceptable to Welsh Labour M.P.'s as to Liverpool Labour councillors. On 13 January 1957 the *Liverpool Daily Post* reported an address by the Merioneth M.P. to the Blaenau Ffestiniog council:

> Mr.Jones said that he had been informed that the establishment of an atomic power station at Ynys, Talsarnau, on the Cambrian coast, could be clinched if the necessary water to serve it could be drawn from the reservoir created at Tryweryn... Mr.Jones explained that his attitude to Tryweryn had been influenced by this link with a scheme which would be situated in Merioneth for the creation of nuclear power... He quoted other Welsh counties which had welcomed industrial schemes and overspills from English cities. 'We must put our prejudice on one side and look at things realistically', he declared. Summing up his attitude to the proposed Tryweryn scheme he said, 'If the county council support the scheme I shall support it, and if they oppose it, I shall do likewise, to the bitter end.'

The speech thus disclosed the CEGB's original intention to build the Trawsfynydd nuclear power station on the coast at Talsarnau which has the most breath-taking view of Snowdon and the mountains of Eryri.

Liverpool's next step was to get a parliamentary Bill

approved by a Town Meeting. The Liverpool Defence Committee did their homework. The meeting was advertised to begin at 2 p.m., but when the town clock struck two it was obvious that the majority of those present in the hall were opponents of the scheme. Alderman John Braddock, the chairman, delayed the opening while he sent urgent demands for the presence of citizen employees of the council. In ten to fifteen minutes they began trooping in, clerks from many departments, some in the livery of the Water Committee. By 2.45 p.m. the chairman felt confident of a majority, and the meeting was allowed to begin. When Dewi Prys Thomas asked from the audience why council employees were there in such numbers the chairman replied that he was not responsible 'for the intelligent interest which the Council's employees take in the affairs of their city.'

There was vigour also in the London Defence Committee which, with the help of S.O.Davies and Raymond Gower, organised a meeting in a large room in the House of Commons to which Welsh M.P.'s of all parties were invited. This was a great embarrassment to the Labour members, who had hoped for a quiet sell-out. An angry Eirene White, chairwoman of the Labour group, gave the Defence Committee an ultimatum that unless it consulted the Labour M.P.'s they would boycott the meeting. They did succeed in dissuading Labour M.P.'s of Welsh extraction who sat for English constituencies from attending. But by now Welsh public opinion was running too high for them to do much more publicly to assist their Liverpool comrades. Nevertheless the wide publicity given to the well-attended meeting in Westminster helped to persuade a number of M.P.'s, including the member for Merioneth, to come off the fence and to join the opposition to the Liverpool scheme. Unfortunately it was too late in the day for the M.P's opposition to have much effect.

In July 1957 the matter came before a select committee

of the House of Lords in its judicial capacity. A little while
before it had rejected, on grounds of natural beauty, a far
smaller and more innocent Manchester plan to extract
water from Ullswater. The Marquis of Reading was in the
chair for the Welsh hearing. Sitting on either side of him
were Lords Baden-Powell, Ashton of Hyde, Milverton and
Greenhill, none of them noted for knowledge of or concern
for Welsh national life. Geoffrey Lawrence, the Liverpool
counsel, conceded that,

> There can be no question that emotions in Wales
> have been aroused.

But he underlined Liverpool's constitutional right to act as
it would do. Wales is a part of England, the Welsh nation
is a nation without a government.

> Liverpool Corporation have to take the constitution
> as they find it. There is at the moment no separate
> Welsh Government; there is no separate demarcation
> of Wales from England from the point of view of
> administration or from the point of view of water
> supplies.

In closing his address he said,

> It is impossible to compare the amount of dislocation
> which would take place in this valley with the dep-
> rivation of water supplies of more than a million peo-
> ple in one of the most vital areas of the whole
> country.

Merioneth County Council contended that the final decision should await the publication of the report of an inquiry
set up by Henry Brooke, Minister for Welsh Affairs. The
purpose of the inquiry was to examine the possibilities of
extracting water for Liverpool from the River Dee or creating reservoirs on one of its higher tributaries. This reasonable request was rejected. Merioneth's counsel also
contended that more than enough water to meet Liverpool's needs could be found by making a reservoir on
either the Celyn or the Hirnant river without drowning
more than two homes. Dewi Watkin Powell on behalf of

the inhabitants of Cwm Tryweryn also indicated other ample water sources where no destruction of homes would be necessary. He emphasised the grave loss to Wales if the cultured Tryweryn community were wiped off the map. Under cross examination Alderman Cain admitted the strength of the opposition but insisted that Welsh nationalists were alone responsible for it. 'They had carried children all the way to Liverpool', he said, 'to sing nationalist songs outside the City Hall.' The 'nationalist songs' were *Hen wlad fy nhadau,* the national anthem, and Elfed's *Cofia'n gwlad,* a great national hymn. At the conclusion of the nine days hearing the Marquis of Reading announced the decision of the House of Lords that the Bill should be allowed to proceed.

The debate on the second reading of the Liverpool Bill in July was opened by Henry Brooke. In his role as Minister for Welsh Affairs he had declared that,

> For many years the distinctive nationhood of the Welsh nation has been felt to be under threat of eventual disappearance through absorption into all the rest of British life... If integration becomes complete, Wales as a separate nation may become forgotten and the Welsh language may die out... It is the opposition of a nation that feels that the fateful hour has perhaps arrived in the fight to keep Wales different from England, and that it is absolutely essential to make a stand on Tryweryn.

but as Minister for Housing and Local Government Brooke argued Liverpool's case, which involved the destruction of an exceptionally cultured Welsh community. He could not believe, he said, that keeping the Welsh way of life alive was a sufficient reason for rejecting the measure. Behind him he had the massive support not only of the Conservative government and most Conservative members but also most Labour Members. As members for Merseyside constituencies Harold Wilson and Barbara Castle, for example, were strongly pro-Liverpool. Welsh Labour M.P.'s, who represented 30 of the 36 Welsh seats, were now, apart from Eirene White, opposed to the measure, in this reflecting Welsh opinion, though still personally lukewarm. Arthur Probert, the member for Aberdare, expressed a typical opinion when he said,

> My personal opinion is that much more harm than good is being done by making this a Welsh versus English issue. It would be just the same to me if Cardiff told Mountain Ash that they were proposing to take over the valley of the Clydach.

But Llywelyn Williams, Abertyleri's M.P., a former active member of Plaid Cymru, did emphasise the exceptional unanimity of the Welsh national and parliamentary opposition. The only Welsh member to vote for the Bill bore two great Welsh names, David Llewellyn. He spoke of, 'a callous indifference to Merseyside', and averred that 'excesses of nationalism are prejudicial to the survival of Welsh.' Yet despite the virtual unanimity of the opposition of the Welsh people and their Members of Parliament, the Bill was given its second reading by a big majority.

Nevertheless, all was not lost. The Bill still had to pass the third reading. Opposition in Wales continued to be strong. But how much reliance could be placed on its parliamentary representatives? In the interim between the second and third reading a meeting was held in Capel Celyn chapel, now under the water, to enable the Merioneth M.P. to give a progress report. Goronwy Roberts, Labour member for Caernarfon, was also there. T.W.Jones gave an account of his bold second reading speech and his unyielding struggle in defence of the Tryweryn community. In order to impress the audience with the admiration this had evoked among the great and good he referred to a letter he had received from no less a person than Jim Griffiths. 'Shall I read it?' he asked Goronwy Roberts who was sitting in front of him in the big pew. 'Yes, by all means, you must read it', said

Goronwy with great solemnity. And while we sat in enthralled silence T.W. slowly drew an envelope from an inside pocket, gingerly extracted an octavo leaf, and in his fruity bass voice read the three sentences of florid tribute from his hero. These left us in no doubt. He had fought a doughty fight. More than that, in his peroration he assured us that he and the Welsh Labour M.P.'s would not cease from their gruelling struggle. They would fight, he said, to the bitter end, 'i'r ffos olaf', to the last ditch.

The last ditch was the third reading of the Liverpool Bill. Alas, on 27 July, a few days before the Bill came before parliament, the *Western Mail's* London Letter reported,

> The Welsh Members, and particularly the Members for North Wales, realise that a final stand would be profitless... The Welsh Members agree that the fight to save Tryweryn is already over.

And so it proved. On the day of the Bill's third reading the *Liverpool Daily Post* reported,

> Intensive efforts were being made in the Commons last night to avoid any debate on Liverpool Corporation's Tryweryn Reservoir Bill when it comes before the House tonight for report and third reading. Mr.Tudor Watkins (Brecon and Radnor, Soc.) who is acting as unofficial Whip for the opponents of the Bill, and Mrs.E.M.Braddock (Exchange, Soc.) who is with Mr.John Tilney (Wavertree Con.) acting as unofficial Whip for its supporters, later agreed to do their best to dissuade anyone from launching a debate on either side... If neither side make the first move a division on third reading will take place soon after seven o'clock.

This was indeed the bitter end. In a few minutes it was all over. 175 voted for the measure, 79 against. The Welsh national community had never been more united, but even a united Wales was powerless. Its opposition was brushed aside. The Tryweryn community was wiped out as completely as the Epynt and Llanwddyn communities had been.

The deep anger in Wales was reflected in an unprecedented way. Within less than a week of the third reading fiasco, Henry Brooke was due to speak from the 1950 National Eisteddfod platform, the greatest honour of the festival week. The Eisteddfod Council cancelled the engagement. No Minister of the Crown had ever been given such humiliating treatment. The depth of Welsh anger was demonstrated in more lawless ways. A number of young nationalists felt that to limit protest to constitutional methods was useless. Dave Pritchard and Dave Walters, two industrial workers from Gwent, released oil from an electric transformer on the Tryweryn site. Elystan Morgan's able defence persuaded the Bala court to discharge them with a fine of £100 each, quickly paid by sympathisers. Emyr Llew Jones and Owain Williams were less fortunate. They were each given a year's term of imprisonment for blowing up a transformer.

My own reaction was that yet another effort should be made to save the Tryweryn community. I published a scheme in pamphlet form which would enable Liverpool to get all the water it needed from the valley of a Tryweryn tributary without drowning a single home and enlisted the help of David Cole, editor of the *Western Mail,* to persuade the Lord Mayor of Cardiff, by then the capital city, to call a national conference in the City Hall, representative of Welsh local authorities and other public bodies. Huw T.Edwards, the most powerful Welshman of the time, was in the chair and John Clement, Secretary of the Council of Wales and Monmouthshire, was acting secretary. The conference unanimously approved the scheme and elected a strong deputation to present it to the Liverpool Corporation. Their journey was in vain. Liverpool's response was flatly negative.

The Lord Mayor's conference was however a national act of importance which proved to be a precedent. Others were called to discuss such national issues as transport and television. Cardiff in the years following its official recognition as the capital of Wales adopted a position of leadership in Welsh national life.

The official opening of Llyn Celyn on a 1965 summer day was a memorable occasion. At the foot of the huge dam a colourful canvas pavilion had been erected to accommodate a host of distinguished guests and civic dignitaries invited to celebrate the opening of the enormous lake. A buffet lunch had been prepared in the pavilion. When their cavalcades of cars arrived the welcome in the hillsides was not to their liking. Some five hundred nationalists had gathered to greet them with jeers rather than joy, and when they assembled in the pavilion the tumult was so great that few distinguished guests could hear a word from the platform. In a few minutes there were no words to be heard. Welsh anger burst forth in a charge of hundreds down the steep slope to the pavilion. The wires of the public address system were severed. The Lord Mayor could be seen opening and shutting his mouth but no sound came forth. His voice was drowned in uproar and soon he ceased trying to speak. Some ropes were cut and part of the pavilion collapsed, doing no physical injury but effectively terminating the ceremony. Liverpool's bright morning ended in a shambles, engulfed by the wrath of Wales.

Although the Tryweryn campaign did not significantly strengthen the national party in Merioneth, where I was the Plaid Cymru candidate, it made a deep and lasting impression on the industrial valleys of Glamorgan and Gwent and on people in their teens in all parts of Wales. Some of the present leaders of Plaid Cymru have said that it was the Tryweryn campaign that awakened their national spirit. Wales has not been allowed to forget the humiliating destruction of the unique valley community. The words COFIA TRYWERYN—Remember Tryweryn, can still be seen, the paint a bit faded, on walls and rocks through the land.

Plaid Cymru lost the fight. The valley was drowned, the community scattered, the water seized. Nevertheless the campaign was seminal. It kindled the national spirit in some of the finest young people in Wales and was doubtless an element in the nationalist victory in Carmarthen the year after the opening of Llyn Celyn. It frightened government into action in Llanwern. It was in 1959 that Aneurin Bevan was converted to the need for a Secretary of State for Wales and that it was adopted as Labour Party policy, and it resulted in the establishment of a new national institution, the Welsh Water Board. This latter was deeply flawed it is true. It had no authority in the mid-Wales area wealthiest in water resources, including the Elan Valley, and it was forbidden to sell the water to English conurbations at a profit which would have reduced the high cost of water in Wales thus helping Welsh industry to compete more effectively.

Plaid Cymru made water a great national issue, important not only in itself but as symbolising the humiliating political and economic position of Wales. It hammered home the fact that one of the richest Welsh natural resources was being exploited without benefit to the Welsh people and that this was possible because of the nation's complete lack of political freedom. Liverpool made a profit of millions from the sale of water taken from Wales free, gratis and for nothing. Birmingham charged people in mid-Wales twice as much for Elan Valley water as was paid by the people of Birmingham. Plaid Cymru campaigned for two rights, for the inclusion of the whole of Wales in the purview of the Welsh Water Authority and for the power to sell water at a profit for the benefit of the Welsh people, just as oil is sold by countries which have the good fortune to possess it. Both demands were fiercely resisted. The party's demand for financial remuneration for Wales from the sale of its water resources was attacked as inhumane. Was not water a free gift from God like the air we breathe, not a commodity to be bought and sold on the market? The concept of Wales benefiting financially from its water resources was castigated as immoral. Consequently our country has been totally denied benefit from the enormous quantities of water taken by wealthy English conurbations.

The water issue provided a further humiliating example of Welsh political subjection in 1989 when Welsh water was privatised in the teeth of strong resistance from 31 of the 38 Welsh M.P.'s. In the decades when Welsh nationalists campaigned for the right to sell this great natural resource for the benefit of the Welsh people they were berated for selfishly wanting to exploit a free gift from God for sordid commercial ends. In 1989 what had been castigated as venal if the Welsh people had been the beneficiaries became highly commendable when London government seized and sold Welsh water resources as a market product to be bought and sold at immense profit by wealthy individuals. Once again the total absence of a Welsh national democracy was underlined.

A small, short lived, success can be noted as a postscript. The three Plaid Cymru M.P.'s succeeded in extracting the Water Equalisation Act from the minority Labour Government in 1976 which voted £4 million per annum to help adjust Welsh water rates closer to the English level. This small measure of justice was cancelled by the Conservative government in 1980 when the referendum and general election had convinced it that it had nothing to fear from Welsh nationalism. £4 million a year were thus added to the Welsh water bill.

8 / For Work, the Economy and Social Justice

A MAJOR nationalist aim has been to temper the unrestrained economic forces which in the absence of a Welsh government have played such havoc with the social and cultural life of Wales. Nationalists have contended that economics should be subordinate to the needs of the Welsh national community. Saunders Lewis wrote in 1932 that Welsh nationalism's first priority was 'to change the entire system of government and of imperialist capitalism that has made my country the worst hell in Europe today.' Although Plaid Cymru has never come near power, its influence on the economy and social justice in Wales has been far from negligible. Its primary achievement has been to secure government recognition of Wales as a national entity in economic planning and development in the post war decades when planning grew greatly in importance. In the generation between 1920 and 1950 there was no respect for the integrity of Wales in economic planning and development in the post war decades when planning grew greatly in importance. There is every reason to think that the government would have persisted in this attitude until today but for the assiduous campaigning of Plaid Cymru for the recognition of Wales as a unit in economic planning and the newly nationalised industries. If nationalists had not fought, in the face of the jibes of such English party leaders as Aneurin Bevan, for separate Welsh status in government programmes, based on the separate culture and historic identity of Wales, the disintegration of the nation would have advanced more rapidly. The establishment of this basic principle did something to modify the rate of disintegration. Without this, emigration and unemployment would have been still worse. But despite the acceptance of the concept of Welsh planning and all-Wales administration there are still some aspects of economic life, such as transport, which are unaffected by it. And Welsh people are still without control over economic development and the necessary infrastructure. We have a strong Welsh bureaucracy but still no Welsh democracy.

The west European countries whose economies developed most strongly in the 19th century were those which had a heavy industrial base in coal, iron and then steel. Wales was richer in coal and iron ore than any European country, but in the absence of a Welsh government its resources were plundered in colonialist fashion with no attempt at balanced development, and no effort to create alternative employment when miners and iron, steel and tinplate workers were thrown out of employment by the ten thousand, and certainly with no vision of the nation's economy and culture as a seamless web. Unemployed Welsh people in the inter-war years had two choices, to be transferred to work in England or to rot on the dole at home. In 1933, despite the transference of hundreds of thousands, 38 per cent of Welsh workers were unemployed, 223,500 subsisting with their families on a paltry pittance. In this appalling situation Saunders Lewis declared that 'The Nationalist Party's duty is to identify itself with the wretchedness of the Welsh poor... It is these who have the first claim on us today.'

The contrast with the Scandinavian and Baltic countries was stark. They had no great mineral resources, not a ton of coal in their land nor any mineral ores. Yet despite their comparative poverty, not only Norway, Denmark and Sweden but even Finland, Estonia, Latvia and Lithuania, who did not win their freedom from Russia until 1918, achieved balanced economic development. Not one of

Norway's 18 counties suffered a drop in population; nine, of Wales' thirteen did. They suffered comparatively little unemployment in the 20's and 30's. When 223,500 Welsh workers were unemployed in 1933 the number unemployed in Estonia was 17,000. By 1938 it had fallen to 2,750. And unlike Welsh communities, Estonian communities were not decimated by transfer of labour.

The enormity of mass unemployment and poverty in the inter-war years, such a gross affront to the human person, closed the eyes of those who thought in Anglo British terms to the erosion of Welsh national life, and closed their ears to solutions proposed by Welsh nationalists who believed that the Welsh economy should be fashioned to serve the nation of Wales rather than the needs of the Anglo British state. They demanded a Welsh government to do the job. The value of self-government had been recognised by Keir Hardie's ILP and the young Labour Party, which declared in its 1918 conference,

> Labour believes in self-government. The Labour Party is pledged to a scheme of statutory legislatures for Scotland, Wales and even England, as well as for Ireland.

Arthur Henderson, as we have seen, expressed his enthusiastic support. The Labour 1929 conference repeated its pledge to Scotland and Wales. This was the last time it did so. From 1931 on Labour has dismissed self-government out of hand, not because it would not be good for Wales but because it would not be good for the Labour Party. The welfare of Wales was sacrificed on the altar of party interests. The Conservative Party has always rejected it. In 1959, Henry Brooke, Minister for Welsh Affairs, declared that it

> would drive the Welsh standard of living down like the Gadarene swine not into the Sea of Galiliee but into the Dead Sea of dire poverty.

The nationalist attitude to the fundamental principles of

economic order was set out by Saunders Lewis in the first issue of *Y Ddraig Goch* in June 1926:

> We oppose the capitalist system because it denies the worker freedom and responsibility, and we oppose state socialism because it makes the people wage slaves in one huge capitalist state.

From the outset the party was radically decentralist. Embracing decentralist community socialism, the Wales it sought to create would be a decentralist country where power and property would be spread as widely as possible in a cooperative order.

As early as 1933, when unemployment stood at 38 per cent, the party published a pamphlet by Saunders Lewis which urged the establishment of a Welsh National Development Council to enable the Welsh people themselves to act in face of the terrible crisis of the time. It was a national crisis. The whole of Wales was involved. The situation in the Welsh-speaking rural areas was quite as bad as in industrial Wales, and even worse in some counties. In 1935 unemployment in Anglesey was 45.7 per cent, in Breconshire 50.7 per cent. Community life was debilitated as young people everywhere poured out of the country in search of work, uprooted and footloose. The population of the Rhondda and Blaenau Ffestiniog, for example, has fallen to less that half; the drop in scores of rural areas was even heavier. Nine of the thirteen Welsh counties had a smaller population in 1951 than in 1851. This was true of only one of the 49 English counties, Middlesex. Yet despite the devastating effects of lack of work in Wales London government had no policy to rebuild the Welsh econony. Wales had no government to provide a centre of growth. The English government long-term policy was to build up the English economy hoping that peripheral Wales would eventually benefit as prosperity spilt over. Its sole immediate remedy, the Portal Report's organised Transference of Labour, had dire effects on Welsh industrial and rural communities.

Inevitably, malnutrition and ill-health were a consequence of mass unemployment. A high proportion of the children of the industrial valleys suffered malnutrition. In the five years 1932-37 deaths from tuberculosis in Wales increased by 30%.

Nationalists continually pressed under Saunders Lewis' leadership for power for the Welsh people to act for themselves. They urged that prosperity be planned, but in a decentralist way. An ambitious scheme for reconditioning and slum clearance was called for in the industrial valleys, as well as large-scale development, re-equipment and repopulation of the countryside. The creation of adequate means of transport communication, particularly between northern and southern Wales, was a constant demand. This planning should be initiated by a powerful Welsh National Development Council. It took forty years to achieve anything approaching that. Nationalists urged local authorities, especially in the industrial areas, to take the initiative themselves in reconstructing the economy under the aegis of Cooperative Public Utility Boards on the Belgian model. These were proposed as immediate steps to mitigate the worst of the appalling effects of the depression. But London government took no step at all apart from moving young people out of Wales. The long-term nationalist policy was the creation of a Welsh cooperative commonwealth which had much in common with guild socialism and even with the near-syndicalism of Noah Ablett's *Miners' Next Step*. The main author of the party's policy of decentralised cooperative control, which was adopted in the early thirties, was D.J.Davies, a former miner in the anthracite coalfield who had been active in the ILP before joining Plaid Cymru.

Nationalist pleas made no impression either on the rigid centralist ethos of the Conservative Party or the Labour Party, which in the twenties became the establishment party in southern Wales. No effective action was taken by the London government or by the local councils, almost all under Labour control in the south. The only small positive consequence of nationalist pressure was the decision of the South Wales and Monmouthshire Industrial Development Council to change its name to The Welsh National Development Council. Although this was a not insignificant step forward, as Butt Philips says in *The Welsh Question,* 'The 'Welsh economy' was not accepted in economic and political circles in Wales until the 1960's'. The idea of Wales as an economic entity was long ridiculed. Planning was dominated by the concept of Severnside in the south and an extended Merseyside in the north, with some Birmingham overspill as a sop to the centre. Most of rural Wales was to be a huge, empty park fit for tourists, unspoilt by industry, with primitive road communications to match. But for nationalist tenacity the odds are that Wales would never have been recognised as an entity for economic purposes.

Agriculture was of course the major industry in most of the country. Plaid Cymru gave it priority for social as well as economic reasons. Communities dependent on agriculture were the backbone of Welsh-speaking Wales. A thriving agriculture was therefore vital to the national wellbeing. The party's priority was reflected in an early pamphlet written by Moses Griffith, a foremost authority in the field. The main object of its agricultural campaigning has been the defence of the family farm as the basis of agriculture within an integrated rural policy. It has had a constant concern for safeguarding the Welsh farm structure and for making the entry of young people into the profession more possible through low-interest finance and increasing the number of holdings available for rental.

The hideous Welsh experience of the 20's and 30's, unparalleled in severity elsewhere in Europe, impelled Plaid Cymru to persevere in the post-war years with its campaign for balanced economic development. Its model was the Tennessee Valley Authority, the outstandingly successful project of Roosevelt's New Deal. The huge poverty-stricken area covered by the TVA was far bigger than Wales, but like Wales it relied almost exclusively on the production of raw materials, coal and wheat in its case, and again like Wales scarcely any of its raw materials were used in its manufacturing industry. Inspired by a sense of urgency the TVA transformed an enormous region by the creative use of electric power. The vision was that of its Chairman, David Lilienthal, who saw the region as an organic entity, viewing its life and resources, economy and culture as a seamless web. Oh that the WDA had this vision today! The mid-Wales Authority has had a glimpse of it. Industry was diversified and redistributed, agriculture revitalised, infrastructure modernised and culture reinvigorated. But while seeing the problems, resources and culture of the region as a whole, the TVA followed a radically decentralist policy, for which Welsh nationalists had long pleaded, in which power was put in the hands of the people. Decentralisation and involvement of the people were at the heart of the plan. In particular there was close cooperation between the Agency and the local authorities. The spirit of the TVA was expressed in the words, 'If industry doesn't come into the Valley, then we'll build our own industry.'

Nationalists sought to apply the Tennessee Valley Authority pattern to Wales and called for a TVA for Wales in order to prevent depopulation and unemployment and to create a stable society and balanced economy. David Lilienthal himself said of the party's first pamphlet on the issue, *Plan Electricity for Wales* by C.F.Mathews,

> I was particularly impressed with the fact that it is emphasised that in Wales too electrical and economic problems are *indivisible*,. . . the life of the Welsh people cannot be split into compartments. . . no venture can be successful unless the people participate.

The TVA's activities were put in the stream of the region's life, sharing responsibility with the people, not autocratically directing the community from above. This was the Welsh nationalist attitude, in direct conflict with English government in Wales. G.D.H.Cole, the prophet of guild socialism and a heavy influence on many nationalists, said,

> Under absentee control a people neither feels nor has responsibility for its own improvement.

That was the Welsh situation. Harold Laski was the guru of many Welsh socialists at this time, although, because it would not be good for the Labour Party, they did not follow his emphasis on the need to involve people in the nation's government, as in this statement:

> The evidence is too strong on all hands; a nation that is given responsibility for its own destiny, by that means gains a breadth of outlook which it cannot achieve in any other way. Self-respect, vigour and creative energy; all these definitely emanate from self-government.

A TVA for Wales was the centrepiece of nationalist policy in three successive post-war general elections, but London governments of both colours remained unconvinced of the need to create the economic conditions for a strong national life. They saw Wales not as a nation but as a peripheral region of enchanting beauty where people from English conurbations could relax from their daily labours.

The fabric of Welsh national life consequently continued to deteriorate from year to year. With the advantages of small size, a moderate climate and, above all, a talented people Wales should have been in the same league as the Scandinavian nations, one the world's successful countries. Arthur Henderson was right. Given self-government, it could have developed

> its own institutions, its own arts, its own culture, its own ideal of democracy in politics, industry and

social life.

A free Wales could have been a social laboratory of value to many in the world. Without any power of action, choice or initiative, it was the decaying ruin of a nation.

Improving the infrastructure was a constant preoccupation of Plaid Cymru. In the immediate post-war years, when publicly generated electricity had not reached many parts of Wales, it led in the pressure for its extension. It demanded a Welsh Electricity Board which could develop the use of electricity in a creative way. Its case was presented in a series of pamphlets, and when the Herbert Committee was established to reorganise the electricity industry it spent a day in Cardiff listening to the party's evidence, of which the *Western Mail* spoke highly. The one success gained in the field of power was the establishment of a Wales Gas Board, whose efficiency and profitability under Mervyn Jones, 'Jones the Gas', did not prevent the centralisers later abolishing it.

A priority of the party has been its long campaign for a road system designed to serve Wales rather than London and the 'home' counties, and for better roads as a condition of balanced development. Like railways, roads in Wales are built from east to west. Two major south-north highways are a basic necessity, one from Swansea to Caernarfon, the other from Cardiff to Wrexham. They were and are necessary not only to secure balanced development but also to unite the country. Their absence perpetuates the separation of the industrial and rural areas of south and north and reinforced the social and economic divisions caused by the country's mountainous terrain. The quite unreasonably negative attitude of the government to major north-south highways to unite Wales indicates a will to keep Wales divided for political reasons. Plaid Cymru has campaigned for south-north roads for most of its existence. When the idea of a Severn Bridge was mooted the party contended that a dual carriageway from Cardiff to Wrexham would be of greater value to Wales. The Cardiff-Merthyr Tydfil section would have opened up the valleys to industrial development, preventing the decay and depopulation of the valley communities. Consequently when the section from Cardiff to Abercynon was eventually completed it was dubbed Welsh Nash Way.

Government's opposition to a north-south highway was based on two grounds, one that there was no industry near the route to justify the cost. Plaid Cymru contended that it was the lack of industry which made the building a major road necessary. Industry follows the road and is needed to stem depopulation. The magnificent autostrada running from the north of Italy to the south through mountainous territory was built both to induce industrial development and to unite the country. A basic reason for the lack of employment which caused chronic depopulation was the absence of an adequate transport system. An outrageous example is the stretch of 22 miles of road from Carmarthen to Lampeter, which is the first section of the road from Carmarthen to Caernarfon. Only in six places on this narrow road, which has over 60 dangerous corners and bends, can the motorist or lorry driver see over 200 yards ahead. What wonder that the Lampeter area unemployment has been amongst the heaviest in Wales. The second ground for government refusal to build a major north-south road was that it would be snowbound in winter! A truer reason is that Wales is more easily governed when kept divided.

Our insistence on good roads as a condition of full employment and the prevention of depopulation had been so persistent that at the time of the Carmarthen by-election I was dubbed Gwynfor Dual Carriageways. In the years before the election summer motorists would often take hours to do the few miles between Nantgaredig and Carmarthen. A deaf ear was turned to pleas for by-passes and a new bridge. Things changed swiftly after the election.

Harold Wilson came to the town, the first time ever for a Prime Minister to visit it. In an evening meeting which he addressed George Thomas announced that a new bridge would be built immediately. By-passes and better roads were also quickly planned.

Plaid Cymru has been urging in recent years a radical rethink of transport policy in view of the greenhouse effect of the scale of emission of carbon dioxide by road vehicles. A revised policy will inevitably give higher priority to public transport, with a new emphasis on railways, especially electrified railways.

No party has struggled as Plaid Cymru has in the defence of Welsh railways. The mid-Wales line would certainly have closed, and probably the Cambrian line too, but for nationalist opposition. The decision to close the mid-Wales line had been made, and was being implemented by the removal of new signalling and other equipment, when I went to see Keith Joseph, then Minister for Welsh Affairs. He called for maps, spread them over his large desk, and I took him over the route. Then he spoke to Ernest Marples the Transport Minister. The closure decision was reversed. The 1966 Labour Government then decided to close the line. Richard Marsh, the Transport Minister, has described his report to the Cabinet.

> I spoke for 15 minutes at the Cabinet and sat back I confess, with an air of satisfaction. The silence was broken by the voice of the Secretary of State for Wales, one George Thomas, who said, 'But Prime Minister, it runs through six marginal constituencies.'

The line started in Llanelli where Jim Griffiths' majority was over 20,000, hardly marginal. After Ammanford it ran through the Carmarthen constituency as far as the Sugar Loaf tunnel near Llanwrtyd. Carmarthen, in nationalist hands, was the cause of George Thomas' agitation. But it was enough. The line was kept open, Welsh nationalism had notched up another success.

The most scandalous illustration of misgovernment of railway transport in Wales is in the field of electrification. In March 1989 Dafydd Wigley asked the Secretary of State for Transport how many miles of railway line there are in England, Wales and Scotland respectively; and how many miles of these have so far been electrified. In introducing his answer the minister said,

> British Rail maintain the relevant statistics on the basis of the railway regions, so separate figures for Wales and England are not available.

The list given below of the mileage of electrified railway track in fifteen European countries shows that the minister could have obtained the Welsh statistic without undue trouble.

COUNTRY	Miles of Track electrified	Percentage Electified
Switzerland	3,220	99.5%
Netherlands	1,931	68.7%
Sweden	6,995	62.5%
Belgium	2,200	61.7%
Luxembourg	162	60.0%
Norway	2,448	58.1%
Italy	9,095	56.9%
Austria	3,129	54.4%
Spain	6,300	49.7%
Germany	11,501	41.9%
France	11,692	33.7%
England	4,207	25.3%
Portugal	462	12.8%
Denmark	199	8.0%
Ireland	37	1.9%
Wales	00,000	00.0%

British Rail plan to electrify another 245 route miles by

October 1992, none of them in Wales. The possible doubling of the number of vehicles on the roads in the next generation, with devastating effect on road transport and the environment, will compel a reassessment of the need for electrified railways.

If Wales had a National Transport Board, for which Plaid Cymru pressed for decades, to develop and coordinate the Welsh transport system, including not only road and rail but air and sea transport (docks have been a particular concern) the present position would not be the shambles it is.

Transport had an important place in the economic plan produced by Plaid Cymru in the late 60's, the only comprehensive plan ever produced for Wales. The work of Dafydd Wigley and Dr.Phil Williams, it was highly commended by Lord Crowther from the chair of the Royal Commission on the Constitution. It was the kind of plan which a Welsh government would have adopted and which the English government should have adopted. Although the plan produced a little later by the Welsh Office trivialised the need, the Plaid plan did have an influence on government which became evident with time.

Few nationalist campaigns bore obvious immediate fruit, yet in a longer perspective their results are significant. Two basic gains were made without which a national future for Wales would be less possible. The first was the recognition of Wales as an entity for economic purposes. The second was the establishment of the Welsh Development Authority and the Mid-Wales Authority, charged with responsibility for economic development in Wales. This agency, established in 1976, which was vital to the development of the Wales TUC and the Welsh branch of the CBI, was by far the most important fruit of the influence of the party and its three M.P.'s on the minority Labour government. An elected assembly could have been still more important but for the servility of the Welsh people themselves.

Many thousands of jobs have been created through the agency of the WDA and the Mid-Wales Authority, which have been further developed by the establishment of WINvest and WINtech and such subsidiaries as Hafren Investment Finance and Welsh Development Capital. There is no doubt now about the commitment of the Welsh Office to autonomous Welsh economic regeneration. Apart from the WDA the number of jobs created through Welsh nationalist activity is considerable. The 7,000 at Llanwern have been noted in the chapter on Tryweryn. 2,800 are employed by the Welsh Office. S4C employs directly and indirectly 3,500. The most amusing example is the establishment of the Royal Mint at Llantrisant. It was to have gone to the north-east of England, but Plaid Cymru's by-election results in Carmarthen and the Rhondda frightened Whitehall and Westminster. Something had to be done to hold nationalism back. So the Mint came to Wales. Dan Smith, the virtual gauleiter of the north-east, was furious. 'What we need here', he cried, 'are a couple of nationalists.'

9 / Defending Local Government

THE BASIC importance of local government has been emphasised by Plaid Cymru from its first days. It could not be otherwise. In the view of its founders and members power should be shared as widely as possible in a decentralist participating democracy: local power should be extended rather than diminished. From the beginning the party insisted that local government should be local and that small entities ensure the fullest democratic accountability. Local government should be government of, by and for community. The wellbeing of local communities demanded that they should enjoy a measure of autonomous self-government. In his address to the first nationalist summer school in 1926 Saunders Lewis said, 'A free nation is a community of communities. . . freedom is a local thing.' This was the antithesis of fascism, of which its opponents so often accused Plaid Cymru. For fascism, the state was everything. Fascism was a centralist ideology like state socialism whereas Welsh nationalism was radically decentralist. In the party's view the national community and local communities, on which central and local government should be based, should be small enough to have a sense of belonging carried by a sense of history. It was the party's emphasis on decentralisation and the small entity, and the small size of Wales, that attracted the active support of Leopold Kohr, the prophet of the small entity and Schumacher's mentor. His book, *Is Wales Viable?*, published by the party, outlined his philosophy in relation to Wales. If the greenhouse effect which threatens life on the planet is to be countered effectively there must be a return to small scale and local planning, as advocated by Kohr, Saunders Lewis and D.J.Davies, if only to ensure a drastic reduction of road traffic and its emission of carbon dioxide.

The first detailed policy pamphlet published by the party was *Local Authorities and Welsh Industry* which urged local councils to create employment, at a time of lethal unemployment, by establishing cooperative industries to manufacture goods for which the authorities could provide a guaranteed market. Throughout the appalling depression years of the 30's the party called for power for Welsh councils to create employment by supplying the market found in Welsh schools, hospitals and local administrative departments. It contended that capital for a variety of industries could be found through the rates. The examples of continental countries such as Belgium and Switzerland were cited. Swiss communes with only a few thousand population could and did establish industries. But the councils, under Labour control in the south, made no move. Creating employment was Whitehall's responsibility in their view. Consequently hundreds of thousands of Welsh people were transferred to England under the iniquitous Transference of Labour scheme, despite which Welsh unemployment reached 38 per cent in 1933. People were treated as ciphers, drops in a labour pool. Mobility of labour and rootlessness, so destructive of community, were the order of the day.

After the war a quarter of a century's experience on the Labour-controlled Carmarthenshire County Council taught me a lot about Labour's attitude to local government and to Wales. For instance it opposed the cooperation of Welsh councils in an innocuous national association, withdrawing membership from the Association of Welsh Local Authorities, whose efficient secretary was the town clerk of Wrexham. National unity was taboo; class unity was supreme for Labour in those days 30 and 40 years ago. It followed that the creation of a powerful association of Welsh local authorities was bitterly opposed although it was so urgently needed to defend Welsh interests. The Carmarthenshire County Council paid an annual fee of thousands of pounds to the County Councils Association, a Conservative-controlled English body which had no concern for Wales; Scotland and Northern Ireland had their own organisations. When the Welsh sub-committee of the Association supported an elected assembly for Wales the CCA opposed it. We argued, but in vain, for an independent Welsh association to which the Welsh councils paid the whole of their fees, which in the early 80's amounted to £300,000, ample to support a well-equipped office and research staff. Opposition to a strong Welsh association had another more personal reason. Its conferences and committees would be held in Wales, denying council members and chief officers and their wives their week in Brighton or Bournemouth, Buxton or Blackpool, and the monthly trips to London. District councils nevertheless decided to forgo these attractions. They created a Council for the principality, which in 1983 merged with the Welsh Committee of the English Association of District Councils to establish an independent Welsh office with a budget of £70,000. The Welsh counties still remain full members of the English CCA with a sub-committee for Wales. If counties are abolished in the next local government reorganisation this will have the advantage of giving Wales a powerful national united body for Welsh local councils.

True to its decentralist policies, for nearly three post-war decades Plaid Cymru strove to defend the structure and powers of local government on the ground that it should be 'based on community and be local and as closely in touch with the area it administers as possible.' The centralising reformers of the civil service and the English parties were obsessed with boundaries and bigness. The fewer and the bigger the units the easier it was to impose central control. For decades therefore the debate centred on boundaries and ignored powers and finance, the areas where reform was most urgently needed. Tinkering with size and boundaries did not touch the heart of the problem.

The centralisers first showed their hand under the first post-war Labour government, whose nationalisation measures were themselves exercises in centralist state planning. A commission set up by Aneurin Bevan proposed the reduction of the number of Welsh counties from thirteen to four, five or six. In the forefront of the opposition, Plaid Cymru's publication and letters to the councils were well received. In particular its pamphlet entitled *The Challenge to the Welsh Counties* was adopted by the Association of Welsh Local Authorities, which bought a thousand copies. The pamphlet criticised the Bevan plan's wrong-headed obsession with boundaries when there was such need to reform powers and finance. It adduced evidence from other lands, especially Switzerland, Germany and the Scandinavian countries, where local authorities were, and still are, far smaller, stronger and more effective than in Wales. The plan was withdrawn as were two subsequent schemes on the same lines which included both district and county councils.

The Local Government Commission continued to produce similar schemes for Wales up to the early sixties. The constant basic assumption was that the bigger the unit the greater the efficiency and the economy, but no evidence was adduced to sustain it. In its annual conference in Machynlleth in 1967 Plaid Cymru adopted the full local government policy by which it still stands today. But Labour's 1967 White Paper followed the old centralist lines, and was in effect the basis of the disastrous policy adopted by the Heath government in 1971. Alone of the parties Plaid Cymru opposed it root and branch. Its basic postulate was that an efficient county council required a minimum population of 250,000, as if education, by far the most important responsibility of county councils, was superior in Birmingham and Liverpool to Merioneth and Ceredigion. The minimum size for district councils was deemed to be between 50,000 and 200,000. No arguments were presented in favour of these standards.

This was the basic tenet of the calamitous Conservative Local Government Act which reduced the number of Welsh county councils from thirteen to eight and district councils from 164 to 37. Mega-councils were created in Dyfed, Gwynedd and Powys. Dyfed extended from near Machynlleth to Milford Haven (110 miles), Gwynedd from Amlwch to near Machynlleth (100 miles) and Powys from Llangynog in the Tanat Valley to Ystradgynlais in the Swansea Valley (130 miles). The huge new provinces, suited perhaps to canton government on the Swiss model, dissipated the loyalty and sense of community nurtured in the old counties. Though it was claimed for them that they would make for efficiency and cost effectiveness, they proved, as nationalists had predicted, more innefficient and more costly. It was argued that there would be economies of scale: their consequence was more scale than economy.

Even more deplorable than the fate of the county councils was the decimation of district, town and borough councils. Although the councils of such very small boroughs and towns as Llandovery, Llandeilo and Cydweli were despised by centralisers their commitment to the welfare of their communities was admirable and their use of their powers efficient. True they were pathetically small by standards set by London centralisers, but efficient Swiss communes, which have tax-raising and even legislative powers, are often still smaller. These small councils marked the limit of participating democracy for which the nationalists fought. The two thousand people of the borough of Llandovery for example had fifteen councillors with a deep interest in the welfare of the community. Many of the people had a councillor in their street to whom they could turn for help. One member for the whole town on the Dinefwr District Council which meets 14 miles away is an inadequate substitute. The local county council member now serves an area of about sixty square miles. Nationalists contrast this situation with Switzerland which, with less than twice the population of Wales, has 26 canton governments and 2000 communes which have less than a thousand population, less than three hundred in 700 of them. All have a continuous history of centuries of service to their small communities, unmatched in the U.K., where the constant chopping and changing of local boundaries deforms communities. Yet the smallest commune has the same extensive powers as the biggest. All have legislative powers. They can and do establish industries. They can and do own great water and forestry resources. They can and do impose income tax, property tax and even estate tax. As in Sweden and other countries in Europe the small communes can act up to the limit of what they can afford. This is the kind of democracy a Welsh government might have striven to create. To Anglo British centralisers such extreme democracy is ludicrous. The road for them has been to diminish the powers of local government and increase the powers of the central bureaucrats. Whitehall hogs power, said Neil Ascherson, as nowhere else in Europe. That is the system in which the nation of Wales is enmeshed.

In formulating its local government policies nationalists were fortunate in having the counsel of Ioan Bowen Rees, Gwynedd's chief executive officer, a former Plaid Cymru candidate in Merthyr Tydfil, whose book *Government By Community* should be, said Max Beloff, compulsory reading for all those entering upon a career in either central or local government.

Plaid Cymru's prophecies during its vigorous campaign against the form which local government reorganisation took in the early 70's proved all too true. But its councillors found little support for their opposition. In the Carmarthenshire County Council we did succeed in persuading the majority of the Parliamentary Committee to oppose, but I was unable to attend the full council meeting where a large majority composed of Labour and independent members supported the reorganisation. Its result was to increase the centralisation of power, to reduce participating democracy, to make local government less local, to swell costs and to lessen efficiency.

Parish councils in Wales were renamed community councils. Their ranks were joined by many of the old town and borough councils. They were the most local of all councils. A reorganisation scheme which depended on counting heads could not be expected to raise their status and increase their powers although the populations they served were similar to those of Swiss communes. Alone of the parties Plaid Cymru had emphasised their importance and sought to raise their status. It was therefore natural that nationalists should have led in creating a Welsh organisation for them. Like the county and district councils, Welsh parish councils belonged to an English association in which they had a Welsh sub-committee. Its conference and committees met in London. Payment for the long journeys and subsistance they involved, together with the London office and staff, absorbed a big slice of the association's income. When reorganisation renamed parish councils in Wales community councils the word parish was dropped from the name of the English association. It became known as the National Association for Local Councils—NALC. The nation in National was England and Wales. The service provided Welsh councils by this 'National' association left much to be desired. Edward Millward and Gwynn Bowyer, both community councillors, therefore pioneered in calling for an independent Welsh association. When The Welsh Association of Community and Town Councils was formed in 1976 the officers appointed included Isgoed

Williams, chairman; Gwyn Jones, vice-chair; Professor Dafydd Jenkins, chairman and Edward Millward, secretary of the legal department; Melfydd George, treasurer and Dr.Wynne Samuel, who led the association for a decade, secretary. Ioan Bowen Rees was the main speaker in the inaugural meeting. All were members of Plaid Cymru. But the chair was taken by Geraint Howells M.P., and Professor Glyn O.Phillips was elected president. The four vice-presidents were, Geraint Howells, M.P., Liberal, Tom Ellis M.P. Labour, Geraint Morgan M.P., Conservative and Dafydd Wigley M.P. Sir Anthony Meyer M.P. has since been elected a vice-president. Although the leadership was given by nationalists the Association was wholly independent of any party. It is a national organisation which has no party loyalty. As people have increasingly realised that the quality of the assistance it gives Welsh community and town councils is superior to the English association it has won growing support from hundreds of community councillors of all parties or none, from Gwynedd to Gwent. Existing to ensure that Welsh communities are respected and are able to play their part in the European context, it has pressed from the outset for a Welsh office in Brussels. 107 councils were affiliated in the first year; now the number exceeds 300. Its early recognition by the Welsh Office was a vitally important event in its history.

Plaid Cymru had anticipated a further local government reorganisation with the establishment of an elected Welsh assembly. Although the shattering 1979 referendum prevented this, the reorganisation that will accompany the creation of a national assembly in the future will be an opportunity to press for more powers for community councils. A Welsh government could organise power from the base up as in Switzerland.

In the meantime the erosion of local government has proceeded apace in the Thatcher years. Supported by only seven of the 38 Welsh M.P's the Conservative government had no kind of mandate for its uninhibited attacks, which nationalists have fought hard. Its housing policy which massively undermined rented housing, struck at the heart of district council responsibility. In the field of education, the main responsibility of county councils, the right of schools to opt out of the system at the expense of local authority grant, and the centrally imposed curriculum, transferred power from the counties to central bureaucrats. Ratecapping also handed to London bureaucrats local council power of deciding rate levels. Combined with constant fiscal cuts, authoritarian government measures eroded the quality of all local government services, including welfare. The iniquitous poll tax, which Plaid Cymru has fought with determination, was aimed at the financial foundations of local autonomy. The Thatcher period is one of implacable diminution of local decision-making power and accountability. It has proved to be a period of relentless increase in the power of the state, that is, of the central bureaucrats, while diminishing the power of the people in their local communities. These years have heavily underlined the need for Welsh self-government and have convinced many who opposed an elected assembly in 1979 of the case for a parliament for Wales.

10 / The Language Struggle: Mass In-migration

THE SURVIVAL and restoration of the old national tongue has long been a concern of those who care for the quality of life in Wales. A salient feature of Welsh history for a century and more, the struggle has intensified as the pressures on the language have multiplied. It is in a different world from the materialism and market forces that dominate government thinking.

Wales has been the homeland of the Welsh people from time immemorial. A Celtic language has been spoken here for some 3,000 years. When a national community developed during the Age of Saints, a millennium and a half ago, its language was Welsh. Taliesin's 6th century poetry is the oldest in any living European language excepting Greek. The vast majority of Welsh local communities were still Welsh in speech four generations ago. But the status of the language, whose literature had for over a thousand years been a major European literature, was destroyed in a grossly humiliating way by political action. The 1536 Act of the English parliament,

> 'incorporated, annexed, united and subjecte (Wales) to and under the Imperial Crowne of this Realme (England)'.

The Act described the Welsh language, which had been the language of law and government in Wales when French was the language of law and government in England in the centuries after the Norman Conquest, as

> 'a speche nothing like ne consonaunt to the naturall mother tonge used within the Realme (England)'.

The statute enacted,

> 'That there shall hereafter be no difference in laws and language between your subjects of your Principality of Wales and your other subjects of your Realme of England. . .
> Also be it enacted that all justices, Commissioners, Sheriffs, Coroners, escheators, stewards and their lieutenants, and all other officers and ministers of the law, shall proclaim and keep the sessions, hundreds, leets, sheriff's courts and all other courts *in the English tongue;* and all oaths of officers, juries and inquests, and all other affidavits, verdicts and wagers to be given and done *in the English tongue;* and also that from hence forth *no person or persons that use the Welsh speech or language shall have or enjoy any manner of office or fees within this Realme of England, Wales* or other the King's Dominion upon pain of *forfeiting the same offices or fees, unless he or they use or excercise the English speech or tongue.'*

Thus did political action by the English parliament utterly destroy the status of the Welsh language.

Over three centuries later another Act of the English parliament excluded the language from the schools of Wales as completely as it had been from legal and official life. By then, without her own government, Wales was defenceless against unrestrained immigration and the mass emigration of her youth in search of work. Little could be done to strengthen the structure of Welsh life in face of the growing ease of transport, and the development of English press and cinema, radio and television which have invaded homes and destabilised communities and played havoc with the traditional language and culture. The surviving Welsh-speaking communities were almost confined by the 1930's to the south and north west. Even these have been inundated by incomers in the last two decades while young people still have to leave their land in thousands to find work. Those who remain suffer the even greater agony, of which J.R.Jones spoke, of seeing their land leaving them.

Most people think of language as a means of communication and no more. Communication is of course its main function, but it is far more than that. It is the vehicle of the nation's culture, the medium through which the nation's values have been, and continue to be, transmitted, the treasury of the nation's experiences and memories, the mind and memory of the nation. Welsh is the most important formative factor in the nation's character, the one unbroken tradition which belongs to Wales. It is the factor which does most to give the Welsh people deep roots in a long past and a sense of continuity. What has been said of the Irish language is true of Welsh, 'Irish is all we have in common with our forefathers and mothers—it is the one thing that is absolutely, distinctively theirs and ours. It is our only important uniqueness.' Emrys ap Iwan said, 'The Welsh language is the bulwark between us and extinction.' It is the badge of Welsh nationhood, the most essential element in our national identity, the factor on which the continued existence of the Welsh nation depends.

Not all Welsh people recognise that the ancient language of Wales is the condition on which the continued existence of Wales the nation depends. The majority perhaps deny it. They point to Scotland where there is no Scottish language which has been spoken through the whole land, yet where there is a strong sense of national identity. The situations are not comparable however. The sense of Scottish nationhood has never rested on a Scottish language, far more on its history of political independence. Gaelic today is spoken by only one per cent of the people, but as a part of their legacy of independent statehood the Scots still have an independent state church, a separate legal system and ancient universities which ar still Scottish in character. Yet even Scotland, says the Scottish *Claim of Right,* 'faces a crisis of identity and survival.' Wales has nothing but her language. If that were lost there would be little more difference between Wales and England than there is, say, between Yorkshire and the rest of England. A sense of national identity could not long survive. 'Heb iaith heb genedl'—no language, no nation—is the stark truth. This is why the restoration of the Welsh language is so vitally important for all the people of Wales, for those who do not have the language as much as those who do. All have a stake in its survival. Fortunately this is realised by increasing numbers of non Welsh speakers, who see it as central in the struggle for personal and national dignity and identity. Scores of thousands of them are more determined than many Welsh speakers are to ensure its restoration; they insist on a Welsh-medium education for their children. Numbers of incomers also do this and learn the language themselves as well.

At the time of the famous Burgos trial of Basque nationalists under the Franco regime Jean Paul Sartre wrote of the Basque language, which was spoken by only about 20 per cent of the people of Euzkadi,

> If Basque were to become the national language of Euzkadi it would carry within itself all the riches of its past, a special way of thinking and feeling, and would enrich the present and the future. What the Spaniard wants is for it to disappear, and with it the Basque personality... The language is the arrow of Basque culture... If they succeed in destroying the language, the Basque will become the abstract man they want him to be. He will speak Spanish, which is not and never has been *his* language... Once he becomes conscious of colonialism the Basque language revives. For him to speak his own language is a revolutionary act.

For Basque read Welsh. If the Welsh language is destroyed the Welshman will become the abstract man so many want him to be, denationalised, without a sense of national identity.

In the 19th century and the first generation of the 20th the popular intellectual culture of the Welsh *gwerin* was the nation's glory. This was no fantasy. It was the way of life of a significant number of the people, and it was unique. Language and culture were woven together. Where the Welsh language was not spoken the culture was not found. But where Welsh was the people's tongue, in industrial and rural parts, a substantial portion of the population had a lively interest in the things of the mind and the spirit, they thought and read for themselves. For most of the last century Welsh was the language of many of the weekly papers in the industrialised south-east. They had a rich cultural content. *Y Gwladgarwr,* for example, published in Aberdare, had a literary page edited by Caledfryn the best Welsh literary critic of the day, followed by Islwyn, foremost poet of the century, who lived all his life in Welsh-speaking Sirhywi in Gwent. The demands made by the poets on the paper's space were so great that the editor had to impose a twopenny tax on each poem selected for publication. In the quarter of a century between 1859 and 1884 *Y Gwladgarwr* published 46 novels, in Welsh of course, many of them written by working men. The most popular of them, *Y Ferch o Gefn Ydfa,* (The Maid of Cefn Ydfa) which went through twenty editions in its English translation, was one of a number written by Craigfryn Hughes, a Quakers Yard collier. *Mae hen wlad fy nhadau,* the Welsh national anthem, was a product of this people's culture, written and composed on the banks of the Rhondda river by two men of the people, father and son, at a time when the Welsh language was in a far stronger position than were such languages as Finnish, Norwegian and Estonian. Finnish and Estonian literature did not begin until the middle of the 19th century, 1,300 years after the time of Taliesin, and there was no Norwegian literature: Ibsen wrote in Danish. Today the languages of Finland, Estonia and Norway are in an impregnable position and their literatures thrive. The Irish position is of course different, but when the Gaelic League was founded in 1893 only fifty people were literate in Irish. But for self-government the Irish language would have disappeared from the Gaeltachts.

This popular intellectual culture survived up to my time where Welsh was the community language. I was first attracted to the Rhondda by the description given me of its life at the end of the last century, highly romanticised no doubt, by an old miner who had retired to live with his daughter near my home in Barry. He spoke of miners during the midday food break underground teaching their butties the 24 intricate closed poetic metres of *cynghanedd* by chalking them on the back of a big coal shovel. I gained a little insight into this life in scores of visits to 'cultural societies' in Welsh chapels for a quarter of a century, in industrial and rural Wales. Big audiences enjoyed talks on a wide range of matters. On two visits to Dowlais for instance I addressed audiences of a couple of hundred people. The most popular lecturers could fill a chapel; they were money-spinning events. And almost every Welsh chapel had its choir, drama company and eisteddfod.

In 1959 a volume of contemporary Carmarthenshire poetry, *Awen Myrddin,* was published as one of a series of ten books of county poetry. The 69 poets whose work was selected by the editorial panel included a policeman, railwayman, steelworker, tinplate worker, forestry worker, insurance collector, two carpenters, three grocers, five miners and ten farmers. The two from my parish of Llangadog were the village cobbler and a roadman working for the county council. Poetry was part of the people's culture; poets had an honoured place in the community, though literary culture was not as widespread in the district as musical culture. The annual, sometimes bi-annual, performances of oratorios and masses by the Llangadog choir were exciting occasions. Musical, literary and oral culture were combined in the two-day Eisteddfod and the chapel eisteddfodau.

It was after becoming a parliamentary candidate in

Merioneth in 1944 that I discovered the full richness of Welsh language culture in rural areas such as Penllyn. A common way of raising money was to hold a *noson lawen*, not only in village halls but in farmhouses which had large kitchens. Eighty or more people could be packed into these cultural feasts. There was a wealth of harpists and *penillion* singers to draw on. I have described in the chapter on Tryweryn the competition which most amazed me, reciting the biggest number of *englynion*. These demonstrations of popular culture disclosed the richness of the way of life bound up with the Welsh language. It was not found where the language had been lost.

Language has the power of revitalising and even creating a national culture. Finland and Estonia are striking examples. In a Finnish government publication Kirmo Mikkola says,

> The nineteenth century was a period of great national awakening in Finland. A feeling of self-respect was created *by the development of written Finnish* and of national institutions. . . When the Kalevala, the national epic, was composed, the depth of Finnish culture's roots was revealed. Finland *was beginning to move towards its own culture*. (My italics).

The Finnish language was thus the source of the national awakening and the astonishing development of Finnish culture. There was a similar development in Estonia. Neither country had a national literature nor even a literary language, before the middle of the 19th century. In both the language revival led to the creation of a flourishing, many faceted culture and to a powerful national movement which achieved national freedom. Although the advantages of Wales have been incomparably greater our achievements have been immeasurably smaller. The splendid poetry of Taliesin, who flourished about 550-580 A.D., is the oldest non-classical poetry in Europe. From the 6th to the 16th century Welsh literature was one of the great European literatures. For seven of those centuries it was unsurpassed, in poetry or prose, in quantity or quality, except for the period of Dante, Petrarch and Boccaccio in Italy. What could a healthy national pride make of such an immense advantage!

If Wales had been conquered and overrun in the 7th century, as were three of the Welsh-speaking kingdoms of the Old North, Elfed, Gododdin and Rheged, the Welsh language could have disappeared, as it did in the three northern kingdoms, before the early Middle Ages. It was Cadwallon who saved Wales from that fate. Had the language been lost, Welsh national identity would have disappeared as completely as in the Old North. Centuries later Wales faced the peril of being conquered and overcome as completely by the Normans as England had been. The Normans did overrun northern Wales, and build castles as far west as Bangor and Caernarfon, Anglesey and Merioneth, before the end of the 11th century. In the south Rhys ap Tewdwr, king of Deheubarth, was killed in battle near Brecon in 1093 when defending his kingdom against the Normans. On the fall of this great rampart the Normans swept to the western coast, building castles at such places as Pembroke and Cardigan. It was a close thing at the beginning of the 12th century in the whole of Wales. The only part of the kingdom of Deheubarth left to Gruffydd, Rhys ap Tewdwr's son, was the commote of Caio in the heart of Y Cantref Mawr, southern Wales' most defensible area. Gruffydd was a king without a kingdom. But both he and the Welsh of the north under Gruffydd ap Cynan, fought back. Gruffydd's wife Gwenllian attacked the Normans near their Cydweli stronghold, but both she and her eldest son were killed. The youngest of her five sons, Rhys ap Gruffydd, who was four years old at the time of his mothers' death, alone survived to early middle age. At twenty-three the leadership fell on his shoulders. His great military and political abilities enabled him to re-establish Welsh government in the whole of the kingdom of Deheubarth and indeed in the whole of southern Wales as far as the English border. But for this impressive achievement the Normans would have ruled southern Wales as entirely as they ruled England. In those circumstances Gwynedd too would have been conquered far sooner. The Welsh language would have died out in the south as it did in the Old North and as Anglo Saxon did in England. Had that happened the Welsh national identity would have ceased before long. In the event, Welsh remained the language of law and government in independent Wales until the end of the 13th century when French was the language of law and government in England. The memory of this high status of the language helps to explain the superb confidence of Dafydd ap Gwilym and the great poets of the 14th and 15th centuries; and it inspired the bards to sustain the national cause up to and beyond Owain Glyndŵr's long War of Independence in the 15th century.

The 15th century is known in Welsh literature as the Great Century. But it was also the century of Owain Glyndŵr, of the Wars of the Roses, which were largely fought between Welsh armies, and of the Battle of Bosworth in which a Welsh army helped to defeat Richard III and to place the crown of England on the head of Henry Tudor, a man of Welsh descent, probably Welsh-speaking. Thinking that this fulfilled the old prophecy that the Welsh would again repossess their ancestral territory in England and occupy the throne in London, the Welsh aristocracy and squirearchy passively acquiesced in the incorporation of Wales in England in 1536. The basic purpose of the Act of Incorporation however was far more dangerous than political annexation. Its purpose was to assimilate the Welsh nation, to make the Welsh people English. This was impossible as long as the Welsh spoke a different language from the English. So the Welsh language had to go. The Act therefore sought to eliminate the Welsh language, proscribing it as an official state medium. It had succeeded before the end of the next century in anglicising the gentry class almost completely. With their backs turned on the nation and language of Wales they have not produced a single national leader in the last 400 years. Their example was emulated by the bourgeois intellectuals of the 19th century and by the 20th century class warriors, who reneged on Wales their nation as thoroughly as the 17th century aristocrats had done.

The language was embraced by the *gwerin,* who became literate in 18th century when three quarters of the people attended Griffith Jones' extraordinary circulating schools, and produced the leaders of modern Wales. Its hold was greatly strengthened by the industrial revolution. In the middle of the 19th century, when close on 90 per cent of the people spoke Welsh, the interraction of language, religion and traditional culture sustained a strong and distinctive national life. An objective observer at that time might well have prophesied a brilliant national future for Wales, a country of talented people, unusually wealthy natural resources and moderate climate in which people could work through the day and the year. This was not to be. London government's aim was still, in Matthew Arnold's words, 'to render its various dominions homogenous'. Lacking the will to live, the Welsh had no spirit to resist this centralising assimilative policy. The humiliating degradation of the old tongue by the 1536 Act of Incorporation had created an inferiority complex regarding Wales and things Welsh which has dogged them to the present day. In the 19th century their dependence on England and the English, who they adored uncritically, was pathetic. In this condition, so far from showing the spirit of the Finns, Estonians and other nations, they lacked even the moral strength to create an independent national political movement. No attempt was made to modernise Wales on the basis of nationhood. Typical of their cowed condition was that the brutally anti-Welsh system of education was imposed on their children in 1870 without resistance. So far from being determined to achieve national freedom to be fully themselves, despite all their unique advantages they lost the will to live as a nation.

Wales in consequence is still a nation in servitude without a jot of control over the conditions of her national life, which is so rapidly being eroded. Her language, spoken now by only one in five of the people, remains the main condition of national survival. What else is there in Wales but its language which is unequivocally Welsh? National identity cannot be sustained by rugby, choirs and laver-bread. It is essential that the language be restored and that Wales become fully bilingual.

The situation of our Breton cousins has similarities with Wales though it is more desperate. In Brittany, France has followed since Napoleonic times a deliberate policy of destroying the nation by destroying the Breton language. At the beginning of this century the number of Breton speakers was nearly double the number of Welsh speakers. Today perhaps there are no more than a few thousand Breton-speaking children and young people. The national language is still almost completely excluded from the schools and the media. Government policy was bluntly stated in 1929 by Anatole de Monzie, French Minister of Education, 'For the sake of French unity the Breton language must disappear.' This was the policy followed towards Welsh by the English government after the Act of Incorporation. The French government knew that if the Breton language were restored France would sooner or later face a Breton nation demanding the rights that pertain to nations everywhere, but if the language died the Breton sense of national identity would melt away.

Because the national tongue on which the survival of a sense of national identity so much depends is so important to all Welsh persons, whether they have the language or not, its defence and restoration has of necessity been in the forefront of Plaid Cymru's policies. Although the establishment of the national party was based on a rejection of mere cultural nationalism it has always insisted that a strong Welsh language culture enriched the quality of life of all Welsh people. This does not imply sympathy with the repugnant notion of grades of Welshness, which Plaid Cymru totally rejects. It is rather a natural consequence of the party's emphasis on the central importance of culture and quality of life. In the first issue of *Y Ddraig Goch,* July 1926, Saunders Lewis wrote,

> The purpose of politics is to succour the life of man. . . The purpose of the Welsh National Party is not to keep the Welsh language as a fetish in Wales—but to make it possible for any Welsh person to live a full, fine, happy, civilised life.

National freedom is of course the condition of Welsh cultural as well as economic and political health. Although these aspects of social life are obviously inextricably interwoven Plaid Cymru is the only party in Wales to recognise this and to try to weave its political, economic and cultural policies together in a seamless web. In the late 60's and early 70's the New Left shared its concern for culture, as well as much of its social and economic stance, which is one reason why Professor Raymond Williams, who later joined the party, declared in 1970 that Plaid Cymru's place in the political spectrum was with the New Left.

But while Plaid Cymru's strong support of the language is right and inevitable, the electoral price it has paid for its loyalty is heavy. Only a minority even of Welsh speakers understood the importance of the language for Welsh national life, whereas among many non supporters who did not have the language the party's stance has been misunderstood and resented, a resentment for years arduously fanned by George Thomas (Lord Tonypandy), Leo Abse and others. The impression was fostered that Plaid Cymru was a party for Welsh speakers only, so that although the language has been a great source of strength to the party, its electoral progress would certainly have been more rapid if it had abandoned the language fight. But in the eyes even of nationalists who have no Welsh this would be an unforgivable betrayal. The party is united in its determination to continue working for the restoration of our people's ancient tongue.

In the party's annual conference in Bala in 1937 I moved a resolution demanding equality of status for the Welsh language with English in Wales, an ambitious aim which is still far from being achieved. The next year a movement was established indirectly by the party, with Dafydd Jenkins, later Professor, as secretary, to organise a petition demanding the repeal of the statutory provision that made English the only official language in Wales, and for the introduction of 'positive measures which would put the Welsh and English languages legally on an equal footing'. Nearly half a million signatures had been collected when the war put an end to the work, which was done almost entirely by nationalists. The petition was presented to parliament but no government action ensued, nor would there have been any fruit at all but for the Llangadog case 30 months later, discussed in the chapter on the war years.

After Saunders Lewis' 1962 radio lecture on *The Fate of the Language,* the leadership of the language struggle was taken by Cymdeithas yr Iaith Gymraeg, the Welsh Language Society, with full party support. But before the society was formed there was no body but Plaid Cymru to fight. Its struggle for a Welsh language radio service is described in another chapter. Another field was the use of Welsh in local government. In the twenties very few councils of any kind used the Welsh language in their meetings or their administration. Under nationalist pressure the number increased. Numbers of councils in northern and southern Wales decided to conduct their business and keep their minutes in Welsh. These included surprising places such as Mold, within a few miles of the English border, and Trefdraeth (Newport Pem.) on the Pembrokeshire coast. The Gwaelodygarth council on the outskirts of Cardiff kept its minutes in Welsh until the late 50's. This was generally opposed on the ground that the place of Welsh was in the home, the chapel and the eisteddfod; nationalists contended that if it were not used for all purposes it could not survive.

When I proposed a resolution in the Carmarthenshire County Council in May 1949 that Welsh be an official language of the council the reaction was one of shocked disbelief, although only five of the 72 councillors could not speak the language. The others spoke to each other in Welsh inside and outside the council chamber, but once on their feet they became monoglot English speakers. The formidable vicar of Pontiets declared the motion to be nothing but propaganda to glorify Plaid Cymru. 'Enough of that nonsense', he cried. The longest serving Labour member, born and bred in Llansadwrn, one of the parishes I represented, inveighed against 'fanatics who exaggerated the importance of the Welsh language.' He was an internationalist, he said, who looked forward to the day when everyone spoke Esperanto—'That's the sort of socialist I am.' Their internationalism was the reason often given by Labour members against raising the status of the Welsh language and, of course, for their opposition to self-government, but their internationalism, which demanded the suppression of Welsh national life, extended no further than London.

Soon after rejecting the proposal that the Welsh language be given official status, however, the council did agree to my proposal that the accurate form of Welsh placenames be used on signposts outside every town and village, so that such corrupt forms as Llangadock and Llangendeirne, Minke and Mothvey became Llangadog and

Llangyndeyrn, Meinciau and Myddfai. Later the council agreed to place bilingual wording on its buildings and vehicles, and the Standing Joint Committee agreed to put Heddlu on police cars and vans. The latter was removed when I lost the parliamentary seat. These small victories were won in pursuance of Plaid's policy of getting as much Welsh as possible in sight in order to Cymricise the environment. The policy was later energetically pursued by Cymdeithas yr Iaith.

As a rule I would speak in Welsh on the council and give an English resumé in conclusion. The first time I did this a senior non Welsh-speaking member, born in Llandeilo, rose before I had completed three sentences to protest that, 'courtesy has departed this chamber. There are people here who do not understand Welsh'—a reference to the five who did not have the language. Several times I tried to persuade the council to instal a simultaneous translation system, but in vain. The No Welsh Spoken Here rule was applied as rigidly in the council as in Westminster, Wales' only parliament. Eventually an experiment was made in the early 70's after I had spent more than two decades on the council. The Aberystwyth University College simultaneous translation system was borrowed for the occasion, and Mr.Hywel Wyn Jones came from Aberystwyth to act as translator. But the experiment was destroyed by collusion between both sides. I was the only member to speak in Welsh. Later the cost of installing a simultaneous translation system was calculated. When the clerk announced that it would cost £3,000 an indignant Labour member jumped to his feet and shouted, '£3,000 Mr. Chairman! For £3,000 we could get a new urinal in Blank street, Betws.' We are still light years away from adapting ourselves to being a bilingual nation and it is the old tongue which is degraded in consequence.

The low esteem in which the language was held by even Welsh-speaking councillors was demonstrated by their hostility to its use in administration. Eileen and Trefor Beasley's struggle for rate demands in a Welsh-speaking district is a dramatic example. Twelve times the Beasleys were taken before the courts. Three times bailiffs seized furniture from their home to pay fines and court costs. Party members helped to buy their furniture back before they eventually won the day. Another notable Carmarthenshire victory was won when the returning officer in a county council election ruled that the nomination of Gwynfor S.Evans was invalid because it was completed solely in Welsh. The party took the matter to the High Court, which declared the nomination valid and awarded costs against the defendant. An important consequence was the Elections (Welsh Forms) Act, since which all official election forms and posters in Carmarthenshire have been bilingual. It was this case which led to the establishment in 1963 of the Hughes Parry Committee whose report in 1965 led to the Welsh Language Act of 1967. Nevertheless local and central authorities have fought a long rearguard action against granting status to the Welsh language in legal and official life; even such an elementary human right as taking the oath in the witness box in Welsh has had to be fought for. When I entered parliament—Wales' only parliament—in 1966 my request to take the oath in Welsh was refused. Welsh is a foreign language in our parliament.

Nationalists all over the country campaigned for Welsh-medium schools. The first county to establish a system of Welsh-medium primary and secondary comprehensive schools was Flintshire under the leadership of the Director of Education, Dr.Haydn Williams, and his deputy, who succeeded him in the post, Mr.Moses J.Jones, who was a long-standing active member of Plaid Cymru. In Carmarthenshire, when two nationalists held the balance in the council in 1958, we made an agreement with the independents which included the establishment of Welsh-medium primary schools in Carmarthen, Llandeilo and

Llandovery. The latter did not materialise because of the strong local opposition led by the headmaster; a Welsh unit established in his school remained stunted in contrast to Welsh schools which invariably grew. In 1964 the Education Committee agreed in principle to establish bilingual comprehensive schools in Carmarthen and Llanelli, but postponed implementation year after year. It was the new Dyfed Council which eventually acted a decade later.

The spread of Welsh-medium education is one of the success stories of the last generation, especially in the south-east. In the Rhondda for instance in 1951 only 194 of over 16,000 school children spoke Welsh; in Pontypridd the situation was still grimmer. Today 20 per cent of the children of the Rhondda and Taf Elai districts are bilingual and the number grows steadily. Although less than five per cent of them come from Welsh-speaking homes they attend Welsh-medium schools. In Cwm Rhymni there were only 108 Welsh-speaking children in 1961. By 1990, 2,550 attended Welsh-medium schools of various grades. There is a wealth of experience in Wales and in other countries such as Canada, Catalunia and Euzkadi, the Basque countries, to prove that teaching through the medium of a second language gives pupils an academic advantage. Plaid Cymru has made no more important contribution than to awaken and deepen the Welsh consciousness of parents who insist on giving their children roots in the life and language of Wales. No other party has contributed to this. On the contrary, the function of the Anglo British parties has been to weaken Welsh national consciousness.

A little progress has been made in higher education. Degree courses can be followed through the medium of Welsh in Trinity College, Carmarthen, and Bangor Normal College. In consequence of a resolution I moved in the University Court in 1950, a committee was set up to examine the proposal that a Welsh-medium university college be established. St David's College, Lampeter was the site I had in mind. This found no support in the committee, which did however recommend that a number of specified arts subjects be taught through Welsh. Since its acceptance by the Court this policy has been followed in Aberystwyth and Bangor university colleges. A valuable recent development was the establishment of the Centre for Advanced Welsh and Celtic Studies in Aberystwyth. The staff and student body of the University of Wales as a whole, however, have been lamentably anglicised.

In conjunction with the advance of education through the medium of Welsh there has been a revival of interest in the nation's history. Nationalism almost always involves a reanimation of interest in national history, which in turn deepens the sense of belonging and of roots in community. A splendid school of Welsh historians which has risen during the last generation is putting the people in possession of their past. That at least cannot be taken away from us.

It is worth noting the attempt of two nationalist leaders, Dr.D.J. and Dr.Noelle Davies, to establish a Folk School on the lines of the Danish folk colleges which made such a vitally valuable contribution, under Grundtvig's inspired leadership to the regeneration of Denmark in the last century. These colleges, whose students had worked in mainly agricultural occupations for some years, concentrated on the history, literature and music of Denmark, to the immense benefit of the Danish cooperative movement. D.J. and Noelle Davies bought a small mansion, Pantybeiliau, near Gilwern, in 1933 to provide residential courses for unemployed men and women. The success of the project depended on the continuance of unemployment assistance for the students. Twelve months passed before the Ministry of Labour accepted the scheme, and support was withdrawn within a year, forcing the folk school to fold up in 1935. Plaid Cymru later published a book on Grundtvig written by Noelle Davies.

The course of the language struggle was changed in

1962 by Saunders Lewis' powerful radio lecture, *Tynged yr Iaith,* The Fate of the Language. After a penetrating look at the grim language situation he asked,

> Is the situation hopeless? Yes, of course, if we are content to despair. There's nothing in the world more comfortable than despair. Then a man can go on to enjoy living.

He called for revolutionary action in the manner of the Beasleys. This was addressed to Plaid Cymru without naming it. He urged the party to follow a policy of deliberate confrontation with the law which would make it impossible to carry the administration on without the Welsh language. He declared,

> I do not deny that there would be a period of hate and persecution and strife rather than the brotherly love so evident in the political life of Wales today. Only revolutionary methods can succeed. Perhaps the language would bring self-government in its train; I don't know. The language is more important than self-government.

The party felt unable to respond as Saunders Lewis hoped. Nevertheless there was an immediate response among young party members, a group of whom met during Plaid's annual conference and summer school in Pontarddulais to form Cymdeithas yr Iaith Gymraeg, the Welsh Language Society. Although it is thus a child of the party the Society is totally independent of it, frequently embarrassingly so. From time to time its activities have been felt to be injurious to the party's work. Certainly relations between the political and the language wing of the national movement have not been free of friction. The Society has borne the main burden of the language struggle and has injected new vigour into it. Although public reaction to its activities has been hostile as often as not, it has done much to enliven our psychologically subdued national community. What it has not done is to remove the electorally damaging image of Plaid Cymru as a Welsh language party.

Cymdeithas yr Iaith is a direct action society, the longest living movement of its kind in Europe. It is wholly non-violent. Despite frequent provocation from police or public none of its members have ever lifted a finger in anger against anyone. Their self-discipline has been impressive, and their suffering in the cause has ennobled the struggle and helped to stiffen the Welsh backbone. Over a thousand members have been imprisoned. Ffred Ffransis has spent five of the last 15 years in prison; his wife Meinir, who has six children, has spent four terms in prison, two in Holloway. The struggle was infused with intellectual intensity by Professor J.R.Jones who, said Cynog Dafis, 'taught us to see the death of the language as something not merely sad or regrettable, but as a matter of the highest seriousness, as a symptom of the crisis of civilisation.'

The 1965 report of the Hughes Parry Committee, set up in consequence of the Gwynfor S.Evans High Court case to examine the legal status of the Welsh language, led to the 1967 Welsh Language Act which ostensibly gave Welsh equal validity with English. This illustrates the relationship of the language and political wings of the national movement. Previous reports which recommended action in Wales had been pigeon-holed. This happened so often to the weighty reports of the Welsh Advisory Committee in the 50's that the Chairman, Huw T.Edwards, resigned in protest and joined Plaid Cymru. The Hughes Parry report might have met the same fate, or it might have resulted in a wholly innocuous little measure like the 1942 Welsh Courts Act, but for Plaid Cymru's Carmarthen victory in 1966.

The late 60's and early 70's saw the reinvigoration of the Welsh Language Society members, 'whose political imagination had been awakened by the Carmarthen by-election', says Butt Phillips. Enhanced pride in the language as the greatest Welsh national tradition has been an important consequence of most of Plaid Cymru's campaigns, whatever their nature. The effect of political nationalism on literature has been particularly profound. Writing in 1965 Saunders Lewis could state that, 'the majority of Welsh poets and writers, dramatists, critics, have since 1930 been avowed members of the Welsh Nationalist Party. . . It is the crisis of Wales that has given this period its *angst.*'

But despite the deepening crisis of Welsh language and nationhood the complacency of the British establishment remained insuperable, its indifference impenetrable. Writing in 1979 George Thomas, then Speaker of the House of Commons, declared that although the Government was doing everything a government could possibly do, some were still unsatisfied:

> Every country in the world has its nationalist minded section [sic]. Wales has had its fires of nationalism fanned by the language problem. . . The tendency has been to look for scapegoats to blame for the decline in the indigenous language. The English people are a natural target because the language that has substituted Welsh is English. . . Every trace of hostility to Welsh has now disappeared. . . Official policy is directed to doing everything possible to sustain the Welsh language. . . The only threat to the Welsh language today is that the fifteen to twenty per cent who speak it will themselves allow it to fall into desuetude.

This absurd statement by a former Labour Secretary of State for Wales reflected government attitude. It exposed a total ignorance of the perilous position of and lack of sympathy for the language of one of the oldest living literatures in Europe, spoken by 40 per cent of the people in 1930 and 19 per cent in 1980.

The language was plunged in the 70's and 80's into the biggest, most complex and most critical problem it has ever faced by the massive shift of English people into Wales. This created grave housing, economic and social problems in every part of the country. An internal colony, Wales has long been accustomed, as Dr.Phil Williams has said, to immigration and emigration being used as a technique of social destruction. It was the mass movement into the Welsh heartlands, depopulated by emigration of young people in search of work, which threatened the Welsh-speaking communities. But emigration was far from losing momentum as the figures given to Dafydd Wigley in answer to a parliamentary question show. During the seven years 1979-85 the outward migration was:

1979	1980	1981	1982	1983	1984	1985	Total
51,000	54,000	53,000	53,000	52,000	50,000	52,000	365,000

People were thus leaving Wales at the rate of more than a million in 20 years. The inward migration is still heavier. The figures published by the medical Family Practitioner Committee for in-migrants settling among Wales' two and three quarter million people during the six years 1981-82 to 1986-87 are:

1981-2	1982-3	1983-4	1984-5	1985-6	1986-7
65,620	68,600	65,300	69,049	73,037	78,917

The numbers are still rising, causing house prices in Welsh rural areas to increase by 50 per cent in 1989. At this rate a million and a half people will have moved in 20 years into the land where the Welsh and their ancestors have lived from time immemorial, over half the country's total population. The equivalent number of immigrants into England would be 25 millions. Welsh nationhood is put in the direst peril.

It is the mass immigration into Latvia and Estonia which has done most to activate the triumphant small nation nationalism which has regenerated their countries. The regeneration of Wales too is possible if the Welsh people show the loyalty to their nation found in the Baltic countries. A more powerful nationalist party would have won for Wales a parliament similar to the parliaments which have given Estonian, Latvian and Lithuanian patriotism a voice and a focus for action. The national languages are spoken by all the Baltic rural communities, which are free from inundation by immigrants, whereas in Wales in-migrants have flooded into almost all the rural areas which two decades ago were quite solidly Welsh-speaking.

The last of the Welsh-speaking industrial villages of the south are also in danger, even the unlovely villages of west Glamorgan and east Dyfed. Up to fifteen years ago the villages of the anthracite coalfield were solidly Welsh-speaking. Stretching from the top of the Tawe Valley through Cwmtwrch, Cwmllynfell, Cefnbrynbrain, Brynaman, Tairgwaith, Cwmgors, Gwauncaegurwen, Garnant, Glanaman, Betws, Tycroes, Capel Hendre, Penygroes, Gorslas, Cefn Eithin, Drefach down through Pontyberem to Pont Iets and Trimsaran—one thought these mining villages would remain Welsh-speaking until judgement day whatever happened to the rest of Wales. But even these are now imperilled. As for rural areas, the process in Ceredigion is typical. At the beginning of the century 18 of every twenty school pupils came from Welsh-speaking homes, now a little over four in every twenty. The position is not dissimilar in north Pembrokeshire and old Carmarthenshire. In 1936 a survey made of the county, including the towns, made by the Carmarthenshire education committee showed that 84 per cent of school pupils came from Welsh-speaking homes. The drop since then has been catastrophic, particularly in the last fifteen years. Rhydcymerau, in the hills between Llanybydder and Llansawel, which has been immortalised in the books of D.J.Williams, exemplifies the process. In 1988 of the 27 children in the school only one came from a Welsh-speaking home. There were only two Welsh families left in the neighbouring village of Gwernogle. Of the 33 children in the Llanycrwys school a few miles to the north, three were from Welsh-speaking home. There is not one in Cilycwm which I knew a quarter of a century ago as a cultured wholly Welsh-speaking area. One could cite tens of similar examples. Farms and houses, shops, pubs and garages have gone into English hands on a huge scale. Of the 25 rural post offices within a twelve mile radius of Lampeter 22 have English owners. Gwynedd in 1980 had 140 communities where over 75 per cent of the people spoke Welsh. In 1990 there were only 17. If current trends continue there will be only one village in Merioneth where three-quarters of the people speak Welsh at the end of the century.

There is no short term answer to this critical situation, which is largely the consequence of Welsh political servitude and economic marginalisation. The immigrants have poured into a country depopulated by generations of emigration. The unemployment at the root of this resulted from the absence of a balanced national economy. A balanced national economy of the kind called for throughout the years by Plaid Cymru is needed to create employment in all parts of the country, not just near the coastal motorways. The farm structure must be safeguarded and young people must be enabled to enter the industry by means of low-interest finance of rented holdings. As Cynog Dafis, the architect of Plaid Cymru's programme, has insisted a data bank is urgently needed to match career opportunities within Wales with qualifications and aspirations. Because Welsh natives are being forced out of homes by wealthier incomers Plaid Cymru has pressed for a complex of measures to enable them to buy or rent houses. To protect and develop the language the party has urged the adoption of a package of education policies, including networks of language centres to give the language to immigrant children, and for scores of intensive Ulpan Welsh courses for adults throughout Wales with professional teachers, to enable native and immigrant adults to master the language. In addition it urges local authorities to recognise the Welsh language as a key element in the planning process, particularly in the field of housing.

Responsibility for providing financial resources to implement these urgently necessary policies lies on the shoulders of a government which spent £3,085 million to defend the way of life of the 1200 natives of the Falklands. Its reluctance to accept the responsibility indicates the low priority the government of Wales gives the protection of Welsh national life.

The Welsh people themselves lack even the power of action enjoyed by the Swiss canton of Graubunden, which is able to impose a measure of control on in-migration and to execute very costly policies to defend the language and culture of its 22,000 Romansch speakers.

Although the Welsh language, and with it the Welsh identity, are imperilled by the devastating effect of mass in-migration on Welsh-speaking communities, London government is unwilling to spend on the defence of the language more than a fraction of what the government of Euzkadi spends on the restoration of the Basque language. This year Wales contributes about £500 million to the government's enormous expenditure on military 'defence' against some unknown threat by some unknown enemy who poses no threat to the life of Wales. If a tenth of the annual Welsh contribution to the British armaments budget were devoted to the defence of the Welsh language against the in-migration threat its prospects would be transformed.

Plaid Cymru alone of the parties has faced up to the threat posed by massive in-migration with constructive proposals. The language problem is inseparable from the economic situation. The long-term solution is self-government, Plaid Cymru's basic aim. But the party presses for the immediate implementation of a comprehensive package of policies for action not only in the field of junior and adult education, but in economic development and employment, in agriculture and planning, training and housing.

Policy patterns from other countries have been presented.

We lack the will to emulate Israel, where three million Israelis have learnt to live their lives through Hebrew which had been a dead language for more than two thousand years. But the amazing successes in Finland, Estonia and the Basque country, which have different degrees of self-government, won by what Lord Tonypandy would have called their 'nationalist minded sections', should be within reach of the Welsh. The leadership shown by their governments in the field of language makes a Welshman green with envy.

Euzkadi, the Basque country, offers a pattern which could be immediately followed in Wales. When the Basques won a measure of self-government in 1978, after a generation of rule by Franco, only about 20 per cent of their two and a half million people spoke Basque, and of those few could read or write it. Only five per cent of primary school teachers were Basque-speaking. One of the new government's first actions was to pass a comprehensive Language Act, which listed the measures to be taken to restore the national tongue. A Language Board with a powerful secretariat were established to implement them, and the strength of government determination was made manifest by the appointment of no less a person than the country's President as chairman of the Board. Long language courses were organised for school teachers; 1,500 hours of instruction are needed to learn a language thoroughly. By the end of 1987, 8,000 teachers had been released on full pay to attend long courses, with the result that 28 per cent of primary school children were being taught through the medium of the native language—more than twice the Welsh proportion. 90,000 adults were attending language courses, taught by 1,500 professional teachers in nearly 500 language centres, two of which were residential with 50 teachers apiece. Language courses for adults cost over £10 million in 1989. This work was supported by the publication of as many as 200 textbooks a year and hundreds of cassettes and costly videos. In the huge federal university of 42,000 students a quarter of the courses are offered through the medium of Basque: hundreds of university textbooks have been published in the language for this purpose. This effort to restore the language, in comparison with which the Welsh effort is puny, has cost the Basque government tens of millions of pounds a year. It has met the cost gladly because a national Basque future depends on the survival of the ancient Basque tongue. When a nation is fighting for survival its government does not usually count the cost too carefully, in peace or war! Unlike Euzkadi, Wales has a government which has never given a determined lead, never produced a comprehensive plan to restore the wonderfully rich language through which the Welsh people lived their lives throughout their long history until the recent period. The government of Wales, which is also the government of England, has not completely abandoned the policy of the 1536 Act of Incorporation of assimiliating the Welsh people by substituting English for their national tongue. Does it hope in the recesses of Whitehall that mass in-migration will help finally to complete the job?

The heroic language campaigns of Cymdeithas yr Iaith since 1962, which have infused the struggle with new resolve, have been given strong support by Plaid Cymru. A number of successes in the public use of Welsh have been achieved, including on road signs, by British Rail, the post office, banks, businesses, local government, in official forms and of course television. A Language Board has been won and an official Welsh Language Education Committee established to further Welsh language education at all levels, including adult classes. However the status of the language of the oldest living literature in Europe remains low, reflected in Wales' only parliament, where Welsh is treated still as a foreign language; not a word of the old British tongue may be spoken there.

For years Plaid Cymru, alone of the parties, has thrown its weight behind the Cymdeithas yr Iaith demand for a new Welsh Language Act to ensure equality of status and equal validity with English in Wales, in accordance with the United Nations Charter of Human Rights and the resolution of the European Parliament on the languages and cultures of regional and ethnic minorities in European communities. A parliamentary Bill introduced by Dafydd Wigley, given a second reading on 4 July 1986, but denied government support, aimed to secure the right of individual persons to use Welsh when dealing with public bodies, local authorities and central government. The cost would be very small in comparison with the £90 million a year the government spends on promoting the English language abroad.

The inadequacy of the 1967 Welsh Language Act which gave Welsh equal validity in Wales with English in principle but confined it in practice to the courts, has been proved a thousand times. It has never been demanded that Welsh be made the only official language in Wales, which is the status demanded for their languages by the Baltic nations, even by the Latvians who are now a minority in Latvia. The Welsh demand is for equality of status which would give every member of the Welsh public a wholly free choice of using either language in public business without requiring duplication. Documents or statements made in Welsh by an individual or company should have the same status as those made in English. Official insistence on an equivalent English version undermines the role and status of the Welsh language. At the same time documents published by official bodies for public distribution should be automatically bilingual.

This was a basic demand in Dafydd Wigley's parliamentary Bill which also contained clauses requiring public bodies to give employees paid leave to learn Welsh as is done effectively in the Basque country; to place an obligation on public authorities to consider the language in their planning processes; to give parents the right to Welsh medium education for their children, and for children to be able to learn Welsh as a second language; to give the right to make out cheques in Welsh and to speak Welsh in the workplace. We must learn to be a thoroughly bilingual country.

11 / Internationalist Nationalism

HEALTHY internationalism rests on a respect for the right of all nations, whatever their size, to be themselves, enjoying the political and economic conditions of a full national life. In Europe full nationhood enriches European civilisation as well as the lives of individual members of the nation. Plaid Cymru is an inherently internationalist and anti-imperialist party. It aims to free Wales from the shackles of British imperialism so that it can cooperate creatively with other nations in Europe and the world. This was the standpoint of the two great 19th century fathers of Welsh nationalism, Michael D.Jones and Emrys ap Iwan, whose thorough-going internationalism was in stark contrast to the stifling British Imperialism of the day which they despised. The tone was set for the national party in this, as in so much else, by Saunders Lewis who regarded Wales as an integral part of Europe since the Roman period. He thought its history made an ambitious role possible for it as the interpreter of Europe in Britain because,

> The Welsh are the only nation in Britain who have been a part of the Roman Empire. They alone were weaned in childhood on the milk of the West. . . Wales can understand Europe, for she is one of the family.

Maybe he claimed too much, but his purpose, to induce the people of Wales to think of themselves as Welsh Europeans rather than provincial British, was valid. For two decades he strove to immerse Welsh nationalism in European internationalism. The way to protect historic Welsh cultural separateness and to re-establish an international dimension, he argued, was to by-pass England and re-unite Wales with the European tradition.

Irish and French influences helped to make Saunders Lewis a nationalist during his five years military service in the first world war, 18 months of which he spent in Greece after being wounded in France. 'Through reading the literature of Yeats, Synge, Patrick Colum', he said, 'I came for the first time to realise what patriotism and the spirit of a nation are.' Deeply versed in French and Italian literature and culture he saw Wales as a European nation, but his vision was not confined to western Europe. The model of political nationalism he set before Welsh eyes was Tomas Masaryk, President and true founder of Czechoslovakia. 'Masaryk always had two homes, Bohemia and Europe', he wrote. 'That is the only nationalism I can admire.' Tomas Masaryk's nationalism, so much admired by the first generation of Welsh nationalists, is once again alive in Czechoslovakia after being eclipsed for nearly half a century.

Dr.D.J.Davies, a former collier and active member of the ILP, fashioned Plaid Cymru's economic policy on the basis of the cooperative socialism which he had experienced in Denmark, where he became a nationalist and where he met his Irish wife Noelle. Both taught in Danish folk colleges. They helped to turn the party's eyes towards Denmark and the other Scandinavian countries. For years a scholarship financed mainly by Dr.Noelle Davies enabled a member of Plaid Cymru to spend a month in a Danish folk college. A book by Dr.Noelle on the great Danish prophet Grundtvig is among the party's best publications.

Y Ddraig Goch, the party's monthly Welsh language organ, followed a deliberate policy in every issue up to the war of discussing the life and politics of countries in Europe and the world. 'We think it is no idle boast to claim', it said, 'that there is more European thought and European flavour in one issue of *Y Ddraig Goch* than is found throughout the year in papers from Cardiff which depend on echoing the ideas of London journalistic agencies.' The journal's international articles however provoked frequent disagreement in the party. For instance in 1933 Professor A.O.H.Jarman wrote, 'Of course one greatly appreciates statements made by some members, and especially yours [Saunders Lewis the editor] concerning India, Cyprus, Malta, China, France and Germany etc., but I well know that party members are not in agreement with many of them.' However the intention was clearly in line with the purpose of the party which, said Saunders Lewis, was to teach the Welsh to think independently of England in international affairs and to give the nation backbone so that she would stand upright and leap over Offa's Dyke to her place in Europe and the world. The tradition has been maintained. It is for this reason that the examples of Estonia, Latvia and Lithuania, of the Scandinavian nations and of such stateless nations as the Basques and Catalans, have been so frequently invoked.

The internationalist character of Plaid Cymru is as pronounced as its pacific nature. For two generations it has placed before the Welsh people the prospect of Wales as a social laboratory, playing a constructive part in international life with a seat in the United Nations Organisation, and then also an equal place in the European Community. Forty countries in UNO, most of them new, have a smaller population than Wales. Iceland, whose population is smaller than Cardiff's is placed next to India in the General Assembly. The representatives of Wales would sit between Venezuela and Yemen, which came into existence during the last century and a half. It is outrageous that Wales, an old European nation whose civilisation goes back to Roman times, is excluded from the international community. Welsh nationalists have nevertheless supported the struggle of some of these young nations for freedom. Among the liberation movements which it has actively supported in the last two decades are those of the Tamils and Vietnamese, Namibians and Nicaraguans, Basques and Bretons, Kurds and Corsicans. Rarely has its annual conference been held without the presence of more than one delegation from another country. It has been in the vanguard of the Welsh anti-apartheid movement and has given solid support to War on Want Cymru. Plaid Cymru M.P.'s alone expressed sympathy in parliament with Iceland during the Cod War. It is a leading member of the European Free Alliance. Tom Nairn has noted that, 'Welsh nationalism has always been strikingly internationalist in outlook, finding a natural affinity in many movements and personalities on continental Europe.' Nairn contrasts this with Scottish nationalism which has tended in his view to be 'somewhat solitary.' Wanting passionately to join the world, Welsh nationalists see their nationalism as a way of being internationalist.

The internationalism of Welsh nationalists differs markedly from the internationalism proclaimed by the Welsh Labourites I encountered in a quarter of a century on the Carmarthen County Council. The Labour group justified its antagonism to Welsh self-government and any measure of Welsh autonomy on the ground that they were internationalists not nationalists, though they were in fact British nationalists to a man. If I heard that once I heard it a hundred times. Welsh nationalism was usually referred to with the accompanying adjective 'narrow'. Their specious internationalism belonged, as Robin Oakey has said, to the most primitive socialist period, to a tradition known to historians as naïve cosmopolitanism, which was typical of socialist movements in all dominating countries in their early period.

Plaid Cymru has been closely associated with all the Celtic nations, with whom Wales had a particularly close relationship in the post-Roman centuries. The Irish Sea was a Celtic lake traversed by monks, craftsmen and merchants travelling between Wales and Brittany, Ireland and Scotland, which was then largely Welsh-speaking. Professor Gwyn Alf Williams has described St.Davids at that time as 'a veritable Crewe Junction of the sea-routes.' Celtic relations were fostered in our time by the cultural Celtic Congress and by nationalists through the political Celtic League. The Irish national struggle had been a source of inspiration to many early members of the Welsh nationalist party. An indication of the continuing interest was the party's publication in the 50's of a splendid book by Dr.Noelle Davies on James Connolly, who had been joined in the 1916 Easter Rising by Arthur Horner, the fine Welsh Communist leader. In the 40's and the 50's there was a close relationship with some leaders of Fianna Fail. De Valera proved a good friend on a number of occasions. When he made his first stop in Wales on his 1948 world tour Plaid Cymru had the honour of giving him the official welcome dinner in Cardiff.

Cooperation with the Scottish National Party has been long and close. I first met the SNP executive in Edinburgh in 1938, and have addressed its annual conference many times, as have other Plaid leaders. Likewise addresses by SNP leaders in Plaid conferences have been an annual event since Douglas Young's wartime visits. We held a joint rally on Trafalgar Square with the Commonwealth Party, once led by Sir Richard Acland, whose decentralist socialist policies and internationalist attitude were very similar to ours. The relationship with the SNP has now been formalised in an alliance.

We have been able to give valuable, though inadequate, help to Brittany, where France has pursued a policy of cultural genocide. At the opening of this century about a million and a half Bretons spoke the Breton language, which is similar to Welsh. The number has been reduced to about a quarter of a million, most of whom are elderly. The language is still excluded from school curricula and is allowed only half an hour a week on television. During the appalling treatment meted out to Breton nationalists, most of them innocent of any collaboration with the Germans, at the end of the war and immediately after it, we gave refuge to a number of them until the English government expelled them. They found refuge in Ireland, which was honourably open to political refugees. Yann Fouèré, the most prominent Breton leader of the time, found refuge with his family in Wales until expelled. While he was here he wrote a 120 page book on Breton Nationalism which was published by Plaid Cymru. The trial of Roparz Hemon, the greatest of Breton scholars, was the occasion of a notable example of help by Welsh nationalists which certainly saved Hemon from a heavy sentence of imprisonment and possibly saved his life. The Welsh weekly, *Y Faner,* owned by two prominent nationalists, Kate Roberts and Morris Williams, sent Dewi Watkin Powell, later Judge, to cover the trial and gave his reports extensive publicity. The National Eisteddfod Council was induced to send a delegation to investigate the Breton situation: it produced an influential report written by W.J.Gruffydd. A recent example of help was the speaking tour I made in 1983 to publicise the successful campaign for a Welsh television channel in order to improve the Breton television position. In the public meetings I usually spoke in Welsh and was translated into Breton. An account of the tour, containing 150 photographs, was subsequently published. The 20,000 people at a festival which I addressed is an example of the astonishing magnitude of some Breton nationalist events. Welsh nationalists have never been able to organise anything on that scale, or even the 7,000 nationalist rally in Barcelona where I spoke in Welsh and was translated directly into Catalan by Esyllt Lawrence. Not a word of Spanish was heard in the rally.

Plaid Cymru's involvement in European movements has deepened in recent years. In the first two post-war decades it was an active member of the International Minorities Congress, whose secretary, Hans Skadergaard, was a Dane. J.E.Jones, Plaid's general secretary, organised a Congress conference in Cardiff in 1955. This was followed in 1975 by the Bureau of Unrepresented Nations which had an office in Brussels and an independent news agency. Again Plaid Cymru took a leading role. During the last decade the party has been prominent in the activities of the European Free Alliance, a movement of like-thinking parties from 18 stateless nations and historic regions, which has 14 members in the European Parliament in the colourful Rainbow Group. Four Alliance leaders attended Plaid's Glyndŵr Rally in Machynlleth, September 1988, to launch the party's European election campaign. The four, who were MEP's, included Karlos Garatoeca, President of Euzkadi, and Willy Kuypers, who was responsible for the resolution in the European Parliament which led to the establishment of the European Bureau for Lesser Used Languages. Nant Gwrtheyrn, the Welsh language centre established under the leadership of Dr.Carl Clowes and other nationalists, has been made the first European centre for minority languages.

The members of the European Free Alliance have a programme in common to which Dr. Phil Williams, Jill Evans and other Welsh nationalists have made a substantial contribution. This was the basis of the policy on which Plaid Cymru fought the 1988 European election. The party's election campaign exposed the contrast between the narrow Anglo British nationalism of the Conservative and Labour parties and Welsh nationalist internationalism. Whereas Plaid Cymru fought wholly on a constructive European programme, the Conservatives fought largely on an anti-European ticket and Labour's campaign was almost confined to making the election a plebiscite on Mrs Thatcher's domestic record. As usual the election was fought mainly on the television screen, from which Plaid

Cymru was almost wholly excluded. The Anglo British parties shared the London news bulletins and current affairs programmes which reach all Welsh homes. Plaid was not in the picture there at all. Even the publication of its substantial European manifesto was ignored. Nor was there any attempt to redress the balance in Wales, where the BBC gave Plaid Cymru less coverage in comparison with its rivals than in any parliamentary election since 1970. Not even a forum was provided for debate on Wales in Europe. Discussion of this question, the central Welsh issue of the election, was absent from the screen. Even the one Public Account programme which was to have debated the issue was axed because of the veto exercised by the North Wales Tory candidate. The replacement programme, to which Dafydd Wigley was invited, was also cancelled because of a Labour Party veto. Despite the exclusion of Plaid Cymru from television news bulletins and programmes in a television election the party's total vote still gave it third place in Wales.

What could be more natural than that this internationalist party should place equality of status for Wales in the European Community in the forefront of its policy?

12 / Nonviolent Nationalism

'PLAID CYMRU today is one of the most internationalist sections of our peace movement.' So wrote
E.P.Thompson, a foremost leader of the peace movement,
in *END,* the journal of the European Nuclear Disarmament
movement. Welsh nationalism is both pacific and internationalist. It has never used, advocated or condoned the
use of violence in the struggle for Welsh national freedom.
No member of the party has ever killed or injured a person
in the name of national independence. The party has never
swerved from its rejection of violence, which was declared
unambiguously by its annual conference at Swansea in
1937. Its opposition to militarism and imperialism has been
staunch, its support for the peace movement vigorous. The
Swansea resolution has never been challenged. Though the
party is not pacifist its record stands in stark contrast to
the nationalism of the Anglo British parties, inheritors of
the militarist imperialism which involved Great Britain in
78 wars in the last century.

Plaid Cymru's attitude to violence is fully shared by
Cymdeithas yr Iaith, the language wing of the national
movement, which stated in its 1972 manifesto,

> Reverence for life is the fundamental value on which
> all other values are based. Take it away and there are
> no other values left... The core of the matter has
> been stated by Waldo Williams elsewhere, where he
> asserts that the use of violence would betray the
> whole moral strength of the movement and its true
> purpose—the development of civilisation, gentleness
> and love.

No party has a comparable record of inflexible and united opposition, set out long before CND was formed, to nuclear weapons. In 1957 the party's annual conference asked Emrys Roberts, then its assistant general secretary, to promote the establishment of a Welsh nuclear disarmament campaign. He did so and became secretary of the movement which was formed. The subsequently formed CND Cymru has had the party's undeviating support, and Plaid Cymru was solidly behind the nuclear-free declaration of the eight Welsh county councils, which made Wales the first country in the world to declare its determination to be nuclear free.

Whereas the Welsh nationalist party has never once departed from nonviolent means of defending the life and the homeland of the Welsh nation, the Anglo British parties have without exception been prepared to defend British independence and territory through the most extreme violence available. The cluster bombs and phosphorus grenades used in the Falklands War are horrific examples of this. Plaid Cymru renounced all methods of violence to achieve national freedom, but war, in which hundreds of thousands of the enemy have been killed, has been the conventional British method of defending Great Britain's freedom and of setting the bounds of empire 'wider still and wider'. Militarist imperialism has characterised the nationalism of every Anglo British party, though the Conservative Party has rejoiced in it more crudely than the others. Although the system they have constructed has done so much to erode and destroy the national life, language and culture of Wales, Welsh people are forced to pay £500 million a year towards its military 'defence'.

For the last 70 years the Labour party has been the establishment party in Wales. Its reputation has been enhanced among the Welsh people by its pose as the peace party. Yet it was Attlee's Labour government which tried to perpetuate war-time Churchillism by striving to maintain

Great Power status. Great Britain was by then a bankrupt client state of the USA. Its claim to the status of a Great Power was thus based on an illusion. Attlee's Labour government nevertheless built Britain's first nuclear bomb. The perpetuation of delusions about imperial grandeur through the post-war years has been wholly injurious to Wales. Useless for defence, the bomb was a chauvinistic effort to maintain Britain's Great Power status. It was a Labour government under Wilson which carried through the purchase of Polaris. It was Callaghan's government which, still hankering after greatness, doubled the power of Polaris at a cost, at 1977 prices, of £1000 million, and which welcomed the deployment of the Cruise missile in Europe. Kinnock's Labour Party, like Ashdown's Liberal Party, decided that the Trident submarine must be retained. This will multiply the country's destructive nuclear power, although it was already greater than the missiles of the USA and USSR were at the time of the Cuban crisis when people feared for the future of the world. Each Trident has eight nuclear warheads capable of being fired 8,000 miles towards eight different targets, and each warhead has 36 times the destructive power of the Hiroshima bomb which wiped out 140,000 people in one second. The possession of these evil weapons, which have the capacity to murder millions of children and their mothers and fathers, grandmothers and grandfathers, each one innocent and each one of infinite value, implies a readiness to use them if the circumstances are deemed to demand their use.

Labour claims to have a better rearmament record than the Tories. Allan Rogers M.P., Labour's junior defence spokesman, boasted in the 1988 RAF debate that,

> It was the Labour Party in power that decided to enter Nato... It was the Labour Party in power that decided to rearm at the time of Korea... It was the Labour Party in power that decided to develop an independent nuclear strategy.

Labour leadership, a few weeks before the 1989 eastern European revolution, sacrificed its integrity to popularity, declaring its opposition to reducing Britain's enormous expenditure on armaments, even to the average spent by members of the European community, despite the effect on pensions, housing, health service, education, infrastructure and overseas aid. Bruce Kent declared in the 1989 Labour conference that,

> An incoming Labour Government could last five years, yet not destroy a single British weapon, nuclear or conventional, not remove a single foreign base or weapon, and not spend a penny less on defence than the Conservatives, and *still* be working within the dimensions of its policy.

Plaid Cymru has opposed not only nuclear weapons but also nuclear power stations, which were built as much for the purpose of producing material for nuclear warheads as for peaceful power. That is why they were maintained at such an enormous loss. The party maintained its opposition at considerable electoral cost. An incident at the Newtown meeting to form CND Cymru illustrated party attitudes. When I proposed that CND Cymru should include opposition to nuclear power stations in its policy on the ground that they were bomb factories, the Labour delegation threatened to leave the movement if the motion were carried. In order to avoid a split I withdrew the motion.

The only two parties in Wales committed to nuclear and conventional disarmament are Plaid Cymru, which has more than four decades of anti-nuclear activity behind it, and the Green Party. If it is asked why the London parties cling to nuclear weapons, which are useless for defence and whose use would be suicidal, the answer is that they feed the British delusion of Greatness, the hall-mark of British nationalism. Small nations are not afflicted by this longing for greatness. Their way of life is peaceful. Norway and Denmark, Sweden and Finland have threatened no one with war and have not been tempted to build nuclear

bombs. Finland, which shares a 778 mile frontier with
Russia, spends only a third of the British proportion of the
GNP on armament but a greater proportion on the poor,
the pensioned and overseas aid. This is the model to which
Welsh nationalists have looked and which a self-governing
Wales would emulate.

The incubus of Great Britain's military pretensions weigh
heavily on the Welsh people socially and financially. The
strongest economies are those of Japan, West Germany,
Switzerland and the Scandinavian countries which are free
of such pretensions. Even Italy which is not as burdened
by them has overtaken British economic performance. The
high level of expenditure on armaments has been a major
cause of Great Britain's economic weakness. The justifi-
cation for Britain's huge military expenditure has been the
alleged peril of USSR invasion of the West. That was
always as much of a myth as the Yellow Peril of old,
though vigorously fostered for the benefit of the military
industrial complexes of the U.S. and some western European countries. A Russian invasion and attempted occupat-
ion of the west would have led to the collapse of the
Russian empire, as the Russians well knew. Russian
soldiers would have been shot in the back by Poles, Czechs
and others. Certainly the threat to the life and culture,
language and national identity of Wales did not come from
the Russians any more than it had come from Germany,
France or Spain in the more distant past. One has to look
nearer home for that. Even the myth of the Russian peril
has now evaporated. There is no Russian enemy any more.
The Warsaw Pact has collapsed. The Russian Empire is
disintegrating. Yet the warplanes still roar frighteningly
over the hills and valleys, towns and villages of Wales. To
bomb whom? Enough nuclear warheads are still stockpiled
in the west to kill every Soviet citizen twenty times over.
Trident is still being built at a cost of £1,200 million to
which Wales has to contribute her twentieth share. The

huge escalation in nuclear warheads involved in the Trident programme sends a message to Israel and Iraq, South Africa, Pakistan and the Argentine.

When military conscription was imposed, it was fought both in the immediate pre-war and post-war years by Plaid Cymru, which contended that the Government had no mandate to conscript the youth of Wales. Nationalists regarded the conscription of Welsh youth not only as a violation of personal freedom but as oppression by a neighbouring nation which should not be endured. A government which made no attempt to defend the national life of Wales, rather the contrary, had little moral right to impose it. Plaid organised a vigorous campaign of open air and indoor meetings and anti-conscription rallies with bands and banners. In Ystalyfera Arthur Horner, the splendid Communist leader, shared the platform with Wynne Samuel, and I had the honour of sharing the platform with George Lansbury in the Central Hall, Swansea, which was destroyed during the war. Ten thousand people filled the Caernarfon pavilion in an anti-conscription rally organised by J.E.Jones, Plaid Cymru's general secretary. Nationalist opposition was renewed when the post-war Labour government re-imposed peacetime conscription. The Keir Hardie Society was formed to lead the struggle. Men of conscription age who refused to be conscripted on national grounds were sentenced to imprisonment. Chris Rees was given a 12 months sentence. At the time of the Korean War Waldo Williams, the saintly poet, twice Plaid's parliamentary candidate in Pembrokeshire, suffered six months imprisonment for refusing to pay income tax in protest against conscription. Bailiffs had already taken all his furniture, reducing him to sleeping on the floor, before he was sentenced to prison.

Clement Davies, Liberal M.P. for Montgomery, moved an amendment to the Conscription Bill to exclude Wales from the measure, from which Northern Ireland had been excluded. Attacking the amendment, George Thomas (Lord Tonypandy), the former pacifist who renounced his pacifism early in the war, declared,

> There is in Wales a small Nationalist Party... Some of the speeches in support of the amendment were made in order to curry the favour of that party. A number of people in important positions of authority in Wales fear the Nationalist Party greatly, and indeed it has since the war temporarily raised its head. I think it would benefit the people of Wales to destroy this wretched nationalism completely.

George Thomas revelled in the acclamation of the largely English audience of M.P.'s when he made his servile attacks on those who tried to defend his vulnerable little nation. These attacks, made to warm English approval, were a feature of his political life until he became Speaker.

A supreme test of parties' attitude to peace and war came with the Vietnam War, fought horrifically by the United States, 8,000 miles from its shores, against a mainly rural impoverished people. Both the Conservative Party and Harold Wilson's Labour Government gave the USA strong moral support. It was the collaboration of the Labour Government with the Americans that led Professor Raymond Williams, the finest political thinker of the century in the countries of Britain, to resign in disgust from the Labour Party. He joined Plaid Cymru soon afterwards. Supporting the Vietnam War was a bizarre way of illustrating Wilson's maxim that, 'The Labour Party is a moral crusade or it is nothing.' In order to demonstrate our horror and to help to arouse public opinion against the apalling American bombing of Vietnam, a group of pacifists whom I joined tried to get to Hanoi in North Vietnam to stand under the bombs. Three of us, of whom the best known was the noble Michael Scott, whose heroic character had been demonstrated in the struggle against apartheid in South Africa and in Namibia's fight for freedom, were to be given Vietnamese visas in Pnom Penh in Cambodia, as Campuchea was then called. We spent a fortnight in Pnom Penh, visiting embassies to gather information about the obscure situation in both Vietnam and Thailand, from which American forces were threatening to invade Cambodia. American bombing did start in 1969. The country was destabilised and the way was opened for Pol Pot's holocaust in which a million and a half men, women and children were massacred. Pol Pot was defeated by the Vietnamese who installed a democratic civil government. Now however the U.S.A., Great Britain and other western countries are planning the return of Pol Pot to a suffering land which is denied all official aid. American pride, so deeply injured by the Vietnamese, has to be salved. A specialised British contribution is to supply the mines technology which blows off the legs of thousands of women and children in the paddy fields and on the paths. When it became clear that the promised Vietnamese visas would not be forthcoming we returned to London. Although the expedition failed in its main purpose, my part in it did reflect Plaid Cymru's attitude to the Vietnam war.

In the Falklands War, which reflected the strain of militarism and imperialism which permeates British nationalism, Plaid Cymru alone of the parties opposed sending an armada 7,000 miles to the Malvinas, to which Argentina, 300 miles away, had a strong claim. Labour was more jingoistic than Mrs.Thatcher in the famous Saturday parliamentary session. It was they who called most loudly for immediate military action. Michael Foot, a great and noble Englishman, 'rattled one sabre too many'. What Labour demanded Mrs.Thatcher delivered. War was endorsed, negotiation rejected. She would later invoke 'the spirit of the South Atlantic' to Labour's embarrassment, in facing 'the enemy within' in the 1984 miners' strike. Labour's hankering after greatness gave her the chance of trumping the welfare state. 'Britain has not changed,' said Thatcher with Labour approval, 'it remains what it was when it built an Empire and ruled a quarter of the world.'

The population born and bred on the Falklands, a territory almost the size of Wales, totalled 1276 at the time of the Argentinian invasion. Most of them lived lives of deadly dullness in isolated settlements. The young people and those in early middle age longed to get away, to Canada, Australia, Britain, anywhere to escape from the cruel boredom of their existence. They would have jumped at a grant of £50,000 to enable them to settle elsewhere. An honourable agreement involving the withdrawal of the Argentinian forces without bloodshed could have been negotiated through UNO, strengthening international order, but the British government, with the opposition's approval, was determined to demonstrate Britain's military power by achieving a triumphant military victory. The Falklands War has been described as essentially an atavistic throw-back to imperial days, so that when the mediation of Perez de Cuella of Peru promised success, the peace effort was scuttled with War Cabinet approval, and international law broken without compunction, by sinking the Argentinian cruiser, General de Belgrano, with the loss of 365 lives, as it was sailing in the direction of Argentina. This was hailed as a national triumph. GOTCHA cried the gutter press. Hundreds were subsequently killed in the fighting on the islands. Scores of Welshmen paid with their lives for Britain's delusion of greatness.

Defence of 'the British way of life' among the 1276 Falklands natives from whom full British citizenship had been withdrawn, was a major aim of a war which cost far more than has ever been spent in defence of the threatened Welsh way of life. More basically the war was fought to satisfy the yearning for greatness which is a constant characteristic of British nationalism. 'Today', cried Mrs.Thatcher in a vainglorious Downing St. effusion after the Argentinian surrender, 'has put Great back into Britain,' echoing the Labour slogan of a few years earlier.

After the humiliations of the Suez War against Egypt, the
Cod War against Iceland and the U.S. conquest of
Commonwealth Grenada, a triumphant Prime Minister was
hailed as a second Churchill. Little wonder Mrs. Thatcher
was reported to be 'furious' when the Archbishop of
Canterbury excluded Rule Britannia and Land of Hope
and Glory from the St.Paul's thanksgiving service. The
general chauvinistic attitude to the war obscured its contribution to securing the future of Conservative politicians,
which led Brigadier Julian Thompson, second-in-command
of the land forces to say, 'you don't mind fighting for
Queen and country, but you certainly don't want to fight
for politicians.' A great opportunity was lost to strengthen
international law and order by referring judgement of
Argentina's indefensible invasion to the UN and the International Court of Justice.

In order to protect the way of life of a population
smaller than Llandeilo, most of whom were longing to
emigrate, a garrison was maintained in the Falklands at the
cost from April 1983 to April 1988, of £1,544 million. The
total military expenditure in the five years 1982-87,
incurred by a government unmoved by the erosion of
Welsh civilisation, was £3,085 million. At this financial
cost, 'Britain', said Mrs.Thatcher, 'has found herself again
in the South Atlantic', and it was true! A tenth of that sum
would transform the prospects of Welsh national life. This
unnecessary war bore no more relevance to the welfare of
Wales or the world than does keeping Britain Great
through nuclear weapons. The resistance of Plaid Cymru,
the only party represented in parliament to oppose it, was
fully justified.

13 / Campaign for Welsh Television

IT IS inevitable that in a nation without a government, the old national language, and even the sense of national identity should be increasingly eroded by the huge growth of media power; especially of television in the last generation which brought English and American cinema into almost every home in the land for hours a day. When the television structure was created the promotion of the cultural life of Wales was as far from the mind of the government and the television moguls as it was from the mind of the BBC in the early days of radio. Even after the establishment of S4C the usual position in Welsh-speaking homes is that children and adults hear far more English than Welsh, while homes where no Welsh is spoken receive scandalously few programmes in English which reflect the life and culture of Wales. An adequate English-language service for Wales is an urgent necessity. The vast majority of programmes reaching Welsh homes originate in London or the U.S.A. Scores of thousands of Welsh homes receive no Wales-originated programmes at all since their aerials are turned towards English stations. The effect of the situation on the Welsh sense of identity is lamentable. The coming of the most powerful medium of communication ever known to the world made an adequate television service for Wales in both Welsh and English a condition of the vigorous survival of the nation's cultural life and native language.

Plaid Cymru campaigned as strongly for a television service for Wales as it had for a radio service, against an indifferent or antagonistic British establishment. Because the immediate peril was to the Welsh language, priority was given from the middle 50's to the campaign for a Welsh language service. Although in 1960 nearly half the homes of Wales had television sets the BBC broadcast no television programmes in the Welsh language. The party's case was outlined in a pamphlet *TV for Wales*. The support it mobilised among local authorities, religious, cultural and other public bodies culminated in a national conference called by the Lord Mayor of Cardiff under the chairmanship of Sir Cennydd Traherne, Lord Lieutenant of Glamorgan. When a gallant attempt was made in 1959 to create a station which would broadcast Welsh language programmes nationalists gave it their full support; Elwyn Roberts, the party treasurer, found much of the capital. The company was a forlorn hope. Cardiganshire was the only virgin territory in its franchise; the rest of the country was overlap where a new aerial was necessary to receive its signal. Commercial rediffusion companies almost all refused to broadcast its programmes. Its income, which the IBA had calculated would be £750,000, depended on the number of sets capable of receiving its signal. They were worth £4 apiece. When the last transmitter was erected on Moel Famau the total number of sets receiving the signal was 60,000, giving it an income of £240,000. It was forced to sell its franchise to TWW after less than a year's broadcasting. The seven hours programmes a week it had put out had proved popular among those who could receive them. A condition of TWW's purchase was that it broadcast the seven hours; the obligation was later transferred to HTV. This alone justified Teledu Cymru's effort.

From 1971 to 1979 Plaid Cymru's role was to support the campaign fought by Cymdeithas yr Iaith, the Welsh Language Society, to achieve a Welsh language television channel. Through the decade the Cymdeithas moved vigorously from one direct action to another with impressive self-discipline, hundreds of members paying for their actions with imprisonment. At one time in 1972 there were 22 Society members in Risley alone. Gronw ap Islwyn was given a six months sentence for phoning the media with news of those who had climbed masts; Ffred Ffransis was sentenced for twelve months for having a map of the way to the Holme Moss transmitter in his pocket. This followed closely on a three year sentence given him in 1971. Of the hundreds who refused to pay television licence fees some were imprisoned, but others were acquitted by sympathetic J.P.'s without a fine. The activities increased in number in the early seventies. In the first three months of 1973 there were two or three direct actions each week. BBC and independent television studios were broken into all over England, roads were blocked in London, there were demonstrations in the House of Commons and House of Lords. These actions were without exception nonviolent; no injury was done to a single person. Despite frequent provocation from police or public, Cymdeithas members have never raised a finger in anger against anyone in the course of their activites. Because clear evidence of law-breaking could not always be brought against individual members the charge of conspiracy became popular. The success of the Language Society's extraordinary campaign in educating the public was reflected in the growing consensus in favour of a Welsh language channel. In 1973 another conference convened by the Lord Mayor of Cardiff unanimously called on the government to give special attention to the needs of Wales when deciding the future of the fourth channel. The following year a committee established by the University Court reported in favour of a Welsh channel. Commercial interests however continued to fight hard for their corner.

The election of three Plaid Cymru members to Parliament in 1974, which indicated that nationalism was again gathering momentum, helped to persuade the Labour and

Conservative parties of the justice of the case for a Welsh channel. The Crawford Committee, set up by the Heath government, reported in 1974 that the 4th channel 'should in Wales be allotted as soon as possible to a separate service in which Welsh-language programmes should be given priority.' This was accepted by the Labour government. In 1975 the Siberry Committee, established to consider the organisation of the service, reported that BBC Wales and HTV should each contribute 12½ hours to the initial target of 25 hours a week. The government targeted 1982 as the date for the commencement of the service, but action was delayed to await the report of the Annan Committee. Annan confirmed the consensus and recommended that the Siberry proposals be implemented as soon as the government could find the necessary finance. Both major parties had now given the policy their support. In 1978 the Plaid Cymru M.P.'s, on whom the government now depended, extracted a vote of £18 million to enable the IBA to proceed with preliminary engineering and transmission work in Wales. Since the Conservative Party had also declared its support it seemed certain that the long and costly campaign had succeeded. There was therefore no trepidation when Labour fell and was succeeded by the Conservatives who had included a commitment to establish a Welsh channel in their election manifesto and then in the Queen's Speech.

The spring of 1979 had however seen more than Labour's fall. The overwhelming rejection of an elected Welsh Assembly on St.David's Day was the most shameful act in Welsh history. The poor general election result for Plaid Cymru, which lost its Carmarthen seat, was a further blow. Morale was at rock bottom. The government, whose attitude to Wales is determined by its assessment of the potential of Welsh nationalism, assumed that nationalism in Wales was a spent force. In the 70's nationalist growth had helped to persuade the major English parties to respond positively to the Language Society campaign; in the autumn of 1979 the Conservatives were convinced that the Language Society and Plaid Cymru would be too demoralised to react effectively to a volte face in the matter of the Welsh television service however shattering. Therefore it reneged on its promise. In September William Whitelaw, who as home secretary was responsible for television policy, announced in Cambridge that there would be no Welsh channel.

The government was not without its Welsh collaborators, led by Harlech Television under the chairmanship of Sir Alun Talfan Davies. The powerful commercial television lobby did its utmost to destroy the consensus in favour of the Welsh channel. It gave a glossy booklet wide circulation among public figures and opinion formers, winning the support even of *Y Faner,* the prestigious periodical established in 1843, which had for half a century supported Plaid Cymru. When Whitelaw made his announcement the government was confident that there would be no strong resistance. It anticipated that the Language Society's predictable reaction could be easily brushed aside. For the Society, which had fought so heroically for so many years, the announcement was of course a staggering blow. Although it sought once again to rally support for the channel the campaign lacked ebullience.

It was at this critical juncture that Plaid Cymru stepped to the fore, and under Dafydd Iwan's leadership formed a joint working party with the Cymdeithas. At its annual conference in October 1979 it expelled the HTV crew and proclaimed its support for direct action. Peter Hughes Griffiths undertook the organisation of a campaign of non-payment of licence fees by party members. The high point came when three noble nationalists of the older generation showed the depth of feeling in the country by ascending the television mast on Pencarreg Mountain, where they broke into the power room with crowbars, switched off the power and remained until the police came to take them into custody. The three were, Ned Thomas, university lecturer and editor of *Planet,* who had been on the staff of *The Times* and had edited *Angliya,* a Russian magazine published by the London government, and had lectured in Moscow and Salamanca; Dr.Meredydd Evans, head of the University extra-mural department in Cardiff, former professor of philosophy in Boston, former head of BBC Wales light entertainment and the foremost authority on Welsh folk music; Dr.Pennar Davies, principal of the Memorial Theological College, polymath scholar, with doctorates from the universities of Wales and Yale, poet, novelist and distinguished literary critic. Despite these actions the lamp still burned low at the end of the year.

The national party's low morale following the referendum, the general election and the shattering government decision on the Welsh channel convinced me that I would have to take some costly personal action to help restore its spirit. Early in the new year I decided that the action would be a fast which would continue indefinitely unless the government restored its Welsh channel policy. Some party officers and Ffred Ffransis were told of this so that the party and Cymdeithas yr Iaith could prepare to renew activities in a big way. On 5th May I announced that the fast would begin on 6th October, giving Plaid Cymru and the Language Society five months to build up a powerful campaign before Parliament reassembled. The conditions laid down for the channel were: (1) 26 hours a week of Welsh language programmes; (2) at peak viewing hours; (3) in a flow; (4) adequately financed; (5) under independent Welsh control. In face of the common contention that half a million Welsh speakers—about the population of Bristol—could not find the talent necessary to produce an average of 3½ hours programmes of good standard a night, we asserted that the shortage was not of talent but of finance. Together with adequate finance the most basic condition was independent control of the medium by a Welsh institution quite separate from Anglo British institutions. The need for an adequate English language channel for Wales was recognised but the Welsh language channel was given priority because it was so obviously a condition of the survival of the national tongue.

Nobody confidently expected that Mrs.Thatcher's government would change its mind. The Prime Minister had already made a reputation as a lady who was not for turning. On 6th May Cymdeithas members opened their blitz by blocking roads in London and by climbing the railings in front of Buckingham Palace to post a proclamation on them. Throughout the month of May M.P.'s and others in positions of authority were energetically lobbied, evoking considerable positive response. Advertisements were placed in influential journals, including *The New Statesman* and *The Spectator*. Hywel Pennar, Meurig Llwyd, Euros Owen, Angharad Tomos and Wayne Williams were given long terms of imprisonment after the renewal of direct action against television masts. Four more senior party members, Cynog Dafis, Iwan Meical, Maldwyn Jones and Mrs.Millie Gregory, broke into the Carmel mast and extinguished the power. It was on the Lliw National Eisteddfod field, where the HTV pavilion was attacked, that the biggest public meeting was held. The rising morale of Plaid Cymru was reflected in the vigorous reception given Mrs Thatcher when she came to the Welsh Conservative conference in Swansea's Patti Pavilion on 20th July. The hostile spirit of the huge crowd prevented her making a dignified front door entrance. She was compelled to enter by the back door past the toilets and make her exit the same way.

An impressive feature of the campaign was the number of Plaid Cymru members who refused to pay their television licence fees. Peter Hughes Griffiths announced in June that the number was 1,500; by September it was over

2,000. Non-payers had begun to come before the courts in the early summer; by September fifteen had been imprisoned for refusing to pay their fines and the number showed signs of mounting to hundreds. Among those imprisoned were D.O.Davies and Douglas Davies, two former bank managers; 73 year old T.C.Jones spent a fortnight in Walton gaol. The possibility of a thousand respectable people in prison was a great embarrassment to the authorities. The local committees launched by a packed Plaid conference in Aberystwyth in June were now active throughout the country. On 21st July I spent two hours with Nicholas Edwards, the Secretary of State for Wales, in the St.Fagans home of Sir Hywel Evans, head of the Welsh Office, being told why a Welsh channel was an impracticable dream.

On September 1st thousands marched from a rally in Sophia Gardens through the centre of Cardiff. This inaugurated a month of nightly meetings, three of which were held in Scotland. All were packed. Feeling was now running high. A revitalised Plaid Cymru again held the initiative. The press was full of news, letters and articles about the campaign, including surprisingly sympathetic leading articles. *The Times* gave its support and *The Sunday Times* made history by publishing a helpful leading article in Welsh. Interviews with newspapers and periodicals were almost daily occurrences. Perhaps the most influential were the many supportive interviews and articles published in European and American papers and periodicals. The *New York Times* published three, the *Christian Science Monitor* two and even *Pravda* had a piece. *Time* and *Macleans* of Toronto were among the periodicals which gave prominence to the story. The Barcelona daily with a million circulation splashed it over its front page. Television programmes were put out in the USA, Holland, Finland and Germany, and two in Scotland. The case for Welsh national freedom was given

179

unprecedented publicity in the wake of the fight for an adequate Welsh television service.

On the 10th September the Archbishop of Wales, the Very Reverend Gwilym O.Williams, Sir Goronwy Daniel and Lord Cledwyn, 'the three wise men', saw William Whitelaw; and Michael Foot saw him on the following day. The reports of their visits given to me by Sir Goronwy and Michael Foot were not encouraging. Nevertheless a week later, on the 17th, a year after Whitelaw's Cambridge announcement, Nicholas Edwards declared that the government had decided to yield. The thousand strong meeting in Crymych that night was an emotional occasion. The collection for Plaid Cymru totalled £2,100! After yielding, the government's attitude has been completely honourable, fulfilling every one of the conditions we laid down.

But why did the government yield? The answer is clear. The strength of Welsh political nationalism was obviously growing again and threatening to reach new heights. A great national awakening was on the horizon. If I were compelled to fast to the end, nationalism's people power could have become insuperable, with the kind of political consequences we have seen in Eastern Europe and the Baltic nations. A Welsh democracy would be on the way. From the government standpoint the deflation of the nationalist movement was imperative. The government professed a fear of violence, but it could have dealt with that unlikely situation without difficulty. The power of political nationalism is a different matter, as the old imperial government in London knows to its cost. Welsh nationalist people power is one Welsh force that London respects and fears.

S4C is an independent Welsh institution whose impressive success has again demonstrated both the gift for organisation and the talent latent among the Welsh people. Although the number of Welsh-speaking people is little

bigger than the population of Bristol the quality of the programmes has achieved the level of the best in Europe. It
has brought the Welsh language into the modern world in
a way unparalleled in any other Celtic country. At a time
when Welsh-speaking communities are being divided and
scattered by massive uncontrolled in-migration from
England—600,000 in the decade 1980-1990—it is S4C
which does most to hold them together nationally. It is
now a major industry employing, directly and indirectly,
nearly 700 people in the Caernarfon district and about
3,500 in Wales as a whole. It has released a spirit of confidence to venture in independent business. The Barcud
Company for instance, which has built at the cost of £5
million a complex including a £2 million studio at Caernarfon, is the biggest television resources company in the
countries of Britain outside London. Although S4C is far
from guaranteeing the future of Welsh as a community
language, without it the language's hope of survival would
be small indeed.

14 / Campaigning for a
Parliament for Wales

ALL ANGLO British parties are nationalist parties.
Defence of the independence of the British state is the first
imperative for each one; for each, sustaining the greatness
of Great Britain is a dominant aim, maintaining Anglo
British culture a fundamental concern. It is not nationalism
which differentiates them from Plaid Cymru, rather the
character of their nationalism. Anglo British nationalists
give their loyalty to the British state; the loyalty of Welsh
nationalists is given to their nation. Welsh nationalists have
renounced violence even as a means of winning national
freedom; Anglo British nationalists have recoursed to
unlimited violence to defend the state's independence.

Plaid Cymru, whose political aim is national freedom, is
the only independent party Wales has had, the only party
to accept responsibility for the defence of Welsh national
life, the only party to take the fact of Welsh nationhood
seriously. No other party has a sense of Welsh history, no
other is conscious of Wales as an ancient nation, the only
heir to Roman civilisation in these islands, whose
nationhood developed in the Age of Saints. Welsh was the
term used by Germanic peoples for those who had been
under Roman rule; Welschland was their term for Italy.
The nation to which Welsh nationalists give their loyalty
was here 1200 years before Great Britain came into existence. This loyalty is the essence of their nationalism.

The Statute of Wales 1536 declared,

> That this said Country or Dominion of Wales shall be,
> stand and continue for ever henceforth incorporated,

annexed, united and subjecte to and with this Realm of England.

With this Act of Incorporation Wales became a peripheral region of England, a marginalised province of the most highly centralised state in western Europe, a nation devoid of power of choice, decision or action, stateless and powerless. The only parliament Wales has is the English parliament where Welsh is a foreign language; its only government is controlled by the 83 per cent of the U.K. population who live in England. This system has brought a small nation of enormous possibilities to the brink of destruction.

The subjection of Wales could not have persisted if the Welsh people had the will to live as a nation. The roots of the Welsh lack of will to live are found in the Act of Incorporation. In the psychological effect of that Act lies the reason for the Welsh failure to build a national movement to modernise the life of Wales on the basis of nationhood as so many nations have done in and beyond Europe. The Act had a deeper purpose than to incorporate Wales politically in England—Britain did not yet exist. Its fundamental aim was to assimilate Wales to England, to make the Welsh English. This was impossible as long as the Welsh spoke a language totally different from English, 'a speeche nothing like, nor consonant to the natural Mother tongue used within his Realm', are the words of the Act, which was directed towards its elimination. English became the only language allowed in official life and courts of law in monoglot Welsh-speaking Wales. The Welsh language, which had been the language of law and government in independent Wales when French was the language of law and government in England, was wholly excluded from official, legal and public life. No one could hold public office, such as lord lieutenant, sheriff or justice of the peace, unless he spoke English. The J.P.'s, who composed the local government of the country, were drawn from the class who had been the patrons of the bards and musicians. Under the new dispensation if a J.P. spoke Welsh in the course of his duties he was dismissed. That was the measure of the degradation of the language of Dafydd ap Gwilym. Nor was Welsh heard in the churches. The services in the Church of England, the only church in Wales at that time, were wholly English. The language whose literature had for a thousand years been a major European literature was stripped of all status.

The effect of the Act of Incorporation on the language penetrated deeply into the Welsh mind. It distorted the psychology of the Welsh people and destroyed their confidence in matters pertaining to Wales. The Welsh of the 17th century have none of the bubbling confidence described by Giraldus Cambrensis in the 12th century; they wholly lack the confident spirit of the Welsh of Owain Glyndwr's day in the 15th century. This is Gerald's testimony:

> Nature gave all the people, the humblest among the common people as well as the great men, a boldness of speech and a confidence in conversation in the presence of princes and nobles, in all manner of situations.

The status of the language inevitably reflects the status of the people; its dignity is reflected in the sense of personal dignity of those who speak it. The degradation of the national tongue of which they had been so proud inevitably depressed the morale not only of the privileged class but of all the people in everything concerned with Wales. Professor R.M.Jones has said,

> The legal or *objective* inferiority conferred on the Welsh language in the 16th century produced a subjective sense of inferiority in the Welshman regarding his own identity and character: feelings of shame and even guilt evolved... and these gradually settled down into a chronic inferiority complex regarding this one thing, his Welshness.

During the century after the Act of Incorporation examples

multiply of people exhibiting a sense of shame towards their language and their Welsh identity which had been totally absent in the previous thousand years. It continued during the following centuries. For instance, William Williams of Llanpumsaint, M.P. for Coventry, in pleading in Parliament in 1846 for a Commission to inquire into education in Wales, which he hoped would devise a system to anglicise the Welsh, said,

> If the Welsh had the same advantages for education as the Scotch [sic], they would, instead of appearing as a distinct people, in no respect differ from the English.

By the end of the 17th century none of the aristocrats and few of the squirearchy had any Welsh and for 150 years there was not a single Welsh-speaking bishop. The upper class were provincial English-speaking monoglots who had turned their backs on Wales and her language. In the last century it was from this class that national leaders rose in many small stateless European countries which won their way to freedom. The catholic Daniel O'Connell and the protestant Thomas Davis and many others rose from this class in Ireland. But in Wales the class has been completely sterile; not a single Welsh national leader has arisen from it in the last four centuries. This goes far to explain the Welsh failure to create a powerful national movement before the English mass parties became deeply rooted.

By the middle of the last century the inferiority complex concerning their Welshness had infected the growing bourgeoisie, like the William Williams quoted above, and the intelligentsia. When nations elsewhere in Europe were awakening, their inferiority complex caused the Welsh intelligentsia to believe that the language and nationhood of Wales were fated to disappear. That was often their ardent wish. They did not want to be 'a distinct people.' They yearned to be English, sharing the glory of imperial England. In Welsh matters they utterly lacked courage which, said Pericles, is the secret of liberty. Courage, the most handsome of the virtues, was for centuries absent from Welsh national life. A sense of inferiority permeated the people. So it happened that when national freedom movements were arising among the more disadvantaged Finns, Estonians, Latvians, Lithuanians, Hungarians, Czechs, Slovaks, Irish and other nations, even Icelanders, the Welsh were rejecting a national future, craving rather to be embraced more tightly by the English. Without a bourgeoisie or an upper class proud and confident in their Welshness a powerful national liberation movement could not be built.

The inferiority complex in regard to Wales and Welsh matters, which stems from the 1536 Act of Incorporation, was thus far from being confined to the language, although its presence is still obvious there. It affected the whole of Welsh life, economic, social and political. It is still very much with us. One sees it in the hatred of the language among some Welsh-speaking people and in public bodies such as the Ogwr, Lliw and West Glamorgan councils. It was massively present in the 1979 referendum on an elected assembly for Wales. It underlies the Welsh fear of seeing themselves as a self-governing nation. This sense of inferiority immensely complicates the task of those who try to restore a healthy national pride and loyalty, the preliminary conditions of success in the struggle for national freedom. Unlike nationalist parties elsewhere, from Parnell's party struggling against England to the Baltic nations pitted against Russia, Welsh nationalists have had to fight on two fronts, against the English government and establishment but also against their anti-nationalist compatriots.

The policies and the independence of Plaid Cymru, and its arrival on the scene when the English parties were strongly established, have made its task more than difficult among a people lacking confidence in their Welshness. Most people did not want to know of, and often deeply resented, its stand for a government of the Welsh people, by the Welsh people and for the Welsh people. The creation of a Welsh democracy was something which most Welsh people found incredible, even abhorrent.

A Welsh democracy cannot exist without full national status. The constitutional status which the party sought in order to establish a democratic Wales was Dominion status, which became Commonwealth status after the war. It was a status of national freedom, not the absolute sovereignty of independence. According to the Statute of Westminster, nations enjoying Dominion status were, 'free and equal nations, in no way subordinate one to the other in any aspect of their domestic or external affairs', but freely cooperating as members of the British Commonwealth of nations. Dominions acknowledged the Crown as a bond between them. Although the King of England was known in Canada and the other dominions as the King of Canada etc., dominion control of military defence and foreign policy was unfettered. Each was a member of the League of Nations and, after the last war, of UNO.

Plaid Cymru adapted commonwealth status for Wales to the situation in the British Isles where the relations between the 'free and equal nations' would be far closer than between the far-flung countries of the old empire, much closer also than between the Scandinavian nations of the Nordic Union. In 1959, well before the establishment of the European Common Market, it published a substantial pamphlet entitled *Self-government for Wales and a Common Market for the Nations of Britain.* Recognising that complete economic separation of Wales from England was a fantasy this outlined some major implications of the party's commonwealth status policy in the circumstances of the British Isles, where a closely knit confederation should be established. Unlike a federation, a confederation has no strong central government. Switzerland was for years a confederation of closely cooperating sovereign states which controlled their own separate defence and foreign policies. Only in the middle of the last century was a central federal government created in Basle. Although the term Confederation is still used, Switzerland is now a federal country. The Scandinavian states, with their Nordic Council and joint boards, have been moving in the direction of confederalism, as indeed is the European Community.

No passports would be needed for travel between the countries of the Britannic confederation, nor tolls or tariffs. People and goods would move freely between them without let or hindrance. Although each country would be politically separate, economically they would compose one common market. This is the situation which will obtain in the European Community after 1992.

Neither Welsh nor English politicians would face the absence of economic separation implied in Plaid Cymru policies. On the two occasions on which I tried to discuss this with Michael Foot, for whom I have great respect and affection, he cut me down with the words, 'We don't want more division in the world,' words that could have been spoken by Stalin to Latvian or Estonian nationalists or by Franco to Basques and Catalans. The dictators were strongly against more division. It is the attitude of imperialists everywhere when they take the high ground. Many British nationalists who take this line against more division have also opposed more unity in the European Community. Raymond Williams has said, 'The truth is that very few people believe in unity or in division as abstract social and political principles. What most people believe in, simultaneously, is the kind of unity they've got used to and the kind of divisions, separations they've got used to.'

Of course Plaid Cymru's vision of a Britannic Confederation was utopian. Wales and Scotland were peripheral regions without a jot of control over their national life and far from achieving even the slightest measure of self-government. After the war the former totalitarian countries of Germany and Italy were decentralised and federalised. Later, after Franco's day, Spain too was federalised, giving the Basques and Catalans their own governments. Even France established regional assemblies. But the tremendous power of British and English nationalism has ensured that the United Kingdom of Great Britain and Northern Ireland is the most highly centralised state in Europe. Incorporated in and subjected to England since 1536 the nation of Wales is devoid of all power of choice, initiative and action. In these circumstances advance to full national status could only be made step by small step through a process which would begin with first administrative and then political devolution.

In the late forties Plaid Cymru tried to put a Parliament for Wales back on the political agenda after an absence of half a century. It was in the 1890's that Cymru Fydd, under Lloyd George's leadership, had briefly campaigned for a Welsh parliament. It had been sufficiently effective to compel Prime Minister Rosebery to come to Cardiff in 1895 to declare himself in favour of a Parliament for Wales, but it had the advantage that Parnell and the Irish nationalist Party had made Irish home rule a burning issue. During the next five decades the matter was absent from the Welsh public mind; there was no vestige of a popular movement in its favour. Plaid Cymru attempted to restore it as a live issue by organising a campaign for a Parliament for Wales in Five Years, inaugurated in 1949 by a rally in Machynlleth attended by 1,500 people who marched through the town to the sound of bands. This, the first political event of the kind organised this century by a Welsh national political movement, was given wide publicity. A number of rallies and scores of meetings calling for a parliament were held the following year. Pamphlets were published and some of the slogans painted are still faintly in evidence.

The first party to respond to the campaign was the Communist Party, which had supported self-determination for Wales and Scotland since 1939. Its 1950 Welsh programme opens with the words, 'We demand the establishment of a Welsh autonomous state within a British Federal Union.' In 1950 also, Undeb Cymru Fydd, a non-party movement established during the war to defend Welsh cultural life, of which T.I.Ellis was the secretary for 25 years, was persuaded to call a conference to organise a campaign and a petition for a Welsh parliament (Ymgyrch Senedd i Gymru). The Campaign, established at a conference in Llandrindod, called for 'self-government within the framework of the United Kingdom' and for a 'Parliament with adequate legislative authority in Welsh affairs.' With Lady Megan Lloyd George as President it was supported by five Labour M.P.'s despite Labour Party hostility, and by some prominent Liberals, though not one of the three Liberal M.P.'s appeared on its platform. The Conservative Party was of course solidly hostile. The miners, under Dai Francis' leadership, gave their support, but Huw T.Edwards, the biggest Welsh political figure of the time, later to join Plaid Cymru, attacked the movement in a pamphlet entitled *They Went to Llandrindod*.

The active workers in the Campaign for a Welsh Parliament were almost without exception nationalists. For two years it displayed little vitality, but after Elwyn Roberts, the Gwynedd Plaid Cymru organiser, was seconded to organise it there was an infusion of energy. Scores of public meetings, in which Lady Megan Lloyd George was the star attraction, were held in packed halls. In 1953 2,000 attended the supporting rally in Cardiff, organised by J.E.Jones the Plaid Cymru secretary, at which S.O.Davies M.P. spoke. After running with others, carrying a torch from Glyndwr's Parliament House in Machynlleth, Emrys Roberts, then student president in the University College, Cardiff, made a moving entry into the packed pavilion. The concourse then marched through the city centre. A quarter of a million signatures were appended to the petition calling for a parliament. 33,000 signed in the Rhondda valleys despite the hostility of the two local M.P.'s. One of them, Iorwerth Thomas, expressed himself in the hysterical terms not uncommon among opponents of Welsh nationalism, which were widely publicised, when he urged people not to sign the petition for a parliament organised by,

> these mad nationalists... if you read nationalist hysteria against the English... Revenge is their cry... These long-haired scholars skulk in Owain Glyndwr's ivory tower and they are determined to shed the blood of Welsh youth in order to realise their policy of revenge on the English... There was never a high standard of culture in Wales... The generosity of the English treasury is responsible for developing our educational institutions and for raising standards to meet the industrial development of our age.

Despite this kind of opposition, it was calculated that 80 per cent of those approached in all parts of Wales responded positively. Shortage of workers rather than lack of support limited the number of signatures.

The petition was presented to parliament in April 1956. In the previous year S.O.Davies had introduced a home rule bill drafted by Dewi Watkin Powell. Although neither the bill nor the petition made an impression on parliament the campaign had heightened national consciousness and helped to plant the idea of a Welsh Parliament in the public mind for the first time this century. Certainly it did no harm to Plaid Cymru, which fought 11 seats in the 1955 election and gained 45,000 votes as compared with 10,000 votes in four seats in 1951. But it did nothing to draw Labour away from its centralism. The response of the Conservative government to the growth of nationalism was rather more positive.

Three reasons were commonly presented by Tories and

Labourites alike for dismissing Welsh self-government, that Wales was too small to be politicaly viable, too weak to defend herself militarily and too poor to sustain a reasonably high standard of living. D.J.Davies' *Can Wales Afford Self-government* was the nationalists' answer to the last of these contentions. But the nationalist case was fortified in the early and middle fifties by help from a neutral source. Professor Arthur Beacham, who held the economics chair at the University College of Wales, Aberystwyth, had been a fellow student of mine, and was persuaded that it would be an interesting exercise to prepare a statement on the Welsh budgetary position. When this proved too big a task for the time at his disposal he asked Edward Nevin, later professor of economics at Swansea, to undertake the work. More, he found substantial money to finance research assistants. It was in this way that the Social Accounts of the Welsh Economy 1948-52 and 1952-56 were produced. Constructing national income and expenditure estimates for a region in a unitary state was a notable feat never attempted before. It attracted widespread attention. Although the figures were of necessity approximations, within about three per cent, they gave nationalists firm statistical grounds for confidence that a Welsh state would be financially viable.

'The Labour Party was at this time particularly antagonistic towards the claims of Welsh nationality', says Butt Phillips in *The Welsh Question* of the early 50's. Nevertheless the growth of political nationalism obliged them to make some move. The *Western Mail* reported in 1954 that Labour leaders were alarmed at 'The progress of the Welsh Nationalist movement and the effect upon Socialist policy and membership.' The comment was prompted by Labour's decision to revise the constitution of the Council of Wales and Monmouthshire and to retain the post of Minister for Welsh Affairs with a cabinet seat. Iorwerth Thomas, M.P. for Rhondda West, was beside himself, declaring that the special problems of Wales were,

> 'little parish pump problems whose political ripples would not disturb the smooth and tranquil surface of a duckpond outside Wales.'

The consequences of the proposals would be, he said,

> 'the setting up of a little Whitehall in Cardiff... The discussion of Welsh problems must be free from the mental neurosis associated with the virus of nationalism.'

Aneurin Bevan had long before this denied that any special Welsh problems existed. 'There is no difference between a Welsh sheep and an English sheep', he said.

Successive Conservative governments in the 50's responded positively, if not in a major way, to the growth of nationalism. Churchill's government had created the office of Minister for Welsh Affairs in 1952, a post which the first incumbent, Maxwell Fyfe (Dai Bananas), combined with the office of Home Secretary. A useful step was the recognition of Cardiff in the following year as the nation's capital city. Plaid Cymru's performance in the 1955 election quadrupling its 1951 vote, kept the national issue alive. Wales had come a long way from the inter-war situation when there was no Welsh political dimension and not one government recognition of Welsh nationhood. Macmillan resolved in 1957 to appoint a Secretary of State for Wales but was persuaded by bureaucratic pressure to drop the proposal. Welsh nationhood has no more implacable antagonist then the Whitehall civil service. However an independent Minister of State was appointed. But there were few Welsh Conservatives capable of adequately filling an office of state. The first incumbent was Lord Brecon who was plucked from the obscurity of the Breconshire County Council and put in the House of Lords—'one of the most curious appointments since Caligula made his horse a consul', said *The Times*.

1959, when the Tryweryn Campaign came to an end,

was a seminal year in Welsh affairs. In response to the pressure of nationalism the government decided, as the cabinet papers published in 1989 reveal, to site the new steelworks in Llanwern in Wales rather than in Scotland. This reflected the weakness of Scottish nationalism as well as the growing strength of Welsh nationalism. Throughout the 40's and 50's Scottish nationalism has not shown the capacity for growth found in Wales. In the 1959 general election Plaid Cymru fought 20 of the 36 Welsh seats, whereas the Scottish National Party fought only five of the 71 Scottish seats. It was in 1959 that Aneurin Bevan, by far the most powerful Welshman in the Labour Party, accepted the need for a Secretary of State, enabling the Labour Party to put it in its election programme. It is to Bevan's credit that he had proposed in the previous year the setting up of 'separate legislative Assemblies for Scotland and Wales and if necessary for regions in England.' He even used the word 'Parliament'. Contrast Kinnock's attitude two decades later.

The Conservatives continued to establish Welsh political institutions. In 1960 it established the Welsh Grand Committee at Westminster, on which the *New Statesman* commented that it was set up because Wales was a nation but denied power lest Wales behaved as a nation. In 1963 the Welsh office of the Ministry of Housing became known as the Welsh Office, and an economic intelligence section was established there to advise on planning the economy.

In view of the claim of 'good Welshmen' in the Labour Party that Welsh nationhood has been recognised in the party's policies as a result of their pressure, it should be noted that there was no comparable group of Welsh neo-nationalists inside the Conservative Party pressurising the party for its long series of acts recognising the existence of the Welsh nation in the political field. This strongly suggests that the Welsh Trojan horse inside the Labour Party had little influence on Labour's policies. Indeed if the able neo-nationalists had thrown their weight behind Welsh nationalism would not the advance in Labour's Welsh policies have probably been greater? It is not from the inside but by leverage from the outside that a small instrument can move a mass.

Far from dismantling Keith Joseph's Welsh Office the Labour Government in 1964 gave it a far higher status when it established the office of Secretary of State. According to D.Ivor Davies, Chairman of the Glamorgan Trades Council Federation and later chairman of the Wales TUC, this office 'symbolised a developing awareness of nationhood among the people.' Initially its responsibilities were confined to housing, local government and roads, but new functions were added, particularly after Plaid Cymru's performance in the by-elections of 1966, 1967 and 1968. Health, agriculture and primary, secondary and further education were added. Significant powers were transferred from the Department of Trade and Industry. Then it gained the power of negotiating funds directly with the Treasury and was given responsibility for distributing rate support grant among local authorities. The budget of the Welsh Office, which now employs some 2,800 civil servants, approaches £4,000 million—80 per cent of Welsh public expenditure. In it the apparatus of a Welsh state now exists. Its development has done much to neutralise the pressure of Welsh nationalism for a Welsh parliament although the Welsh Office is not answerable to the Welsh people. Democratising this bureaucratic tier of government by making it responsible to an elected assembly was rejected by the people of Wales in the 1979 referendum.

Conservatives had responded to the growing potential of Welsh nationalism in the 50's in the ways described above. Another response was the introduction of a Welsh book grant which led to the establishment of the Welsh Books Council. They also published a circular urging full bilingualism in the schools. After Plaid Cymru's electoral successes in the late 60's David Gibson-Watt, Conservative shadow Secretary of State for Wales, wrote,

> If nationalism gets much support in a general election, pressure on the government of the day will drive it to give concessions to Nationalism, and little by little we shall arrive at the situation where Home Rule is inevitable.

However, the Thatcher years have shown that Welsh nationalism, unlike Estonian, Latvian and Lithuanian nationalism, is far from being strong enough to crack the rigid centralism of the London government. Nevertheless it has compelled the Conservative Party, like the other Anglo British parties, to create a Welsh regional structure. Since 1976 even the Conservatives have held a Welsh annual conference. This has not lessened their determination, which is matched by Labour's, to maintain London's monopoly of power over Wales, a monopoly more rigid than Moscow's monopoly of power over the Baltic nations ever was. At least Estonia, Latvia and Lithuania had parliaments.

Decades of campaigning for a Welsh parliament led to a fresh impetus by the remarkable nationalist electoral successes of the late 60's. The conventional wisdom had been that Plaid Cymru would never win a parliamentary seat, and indeed it had never come within reach of winning one. Winning the Carmarthen constituency against all the odds in 1966 was therefore a rude shock to political society in the United Kingdom, all the greater because the Carmarthen constituency included a considerable industrial belt. This demonstration of life in a nation assumed to be politically moribund astounded people and moved some Labour M.P.'s to action. When Cledwyn Hughes pressed in the Cabinet for an elected council for Wales, Richard Crossman noted in his diary in 1967:

> There are a number of Welsh M.P.'s, headed by the present Secretary of State for Wales, who regard the threat of Welsh nationalism as very serious and

would like to meet it by moving towards something
very like Welsh self-government.

Crossman also noted that these were opposed by most of
the South Wales M.P.'s who 'think any surrender to the
nationalists is an act of cowardly appeasement.' It was not
these however who killed the plan for an elected Welsh
Council which Cledwyn Hughes put before the cabinet in
1965, but rather Willie Ross, the Secretary of State for
Scotland. Since Scottish nationalism was still too weak to
compel the Labour Party to move forward in Scotland,
Ross was strong enough to prevent the development of
Scottish national political institutions. It was this which
made development in Wales totally unacceptable to him.

However Winnie Ewing's unexpected victory against
Labour in Hamilton 18 months after the Carmarthen election transformed the situation and took Scotland a leap forward towards autonomy. In the year of the Hamilton
victory Vic Davies reduced the Labour majority in
Rhondda West from 16,888 to 2,306, and in the following
year Phil Williams cut Labour's majority of 21,148 to
1,874. Plaid Cymru's proportion of the vote was higher in
the Rhondda and Caerffili than in Carmarthen. Both these
amazing results were achieved in industrial non-Welsh-
speaking constituencies. A new political era had been
inaugurated in Wales by the Carmarthen election, whose
consequences are still rumbling, threatening to lead in time
to a constitutional change as revolutionary as that of the
Baltic nations.

It was in these circumstances that James Griffiths
expressed his fear that Plaid Cymru could displace Labour
as the biggest party in Wales. Labour was therefore compelled to defuse the nationalist threat to its hegemony. It
did so in two ways. The first was a jamboree which
exploited the powerful emotional appeal, which is at the
heart of Anglo British nationalism, of the English crown
and royal family. The investiture of the Prince of Wales in

Caernarfon Castle in 1969 was a hugely successful public relations exercise seen on the television screen by hundreds of millions throughout the world. It contributed to halting the advance of Welsh nationalism and to inflating the Anglo British nationalism which has stunted the Welsh spirit ever since the Napoleonic wars. George Thomas, whose term as Secretary of State was marked, said *Planet,* by 'awful provincial shabbiness', made no attempt to hide his delight at the prospect of his nation's freedom movement being engulfed in a tide of sentimental royalism. Plaid Cymru thought it wise to keep its distance from the investiture rather than to oppose it vigorously; it had burnt its fingers at the time of George V's coronation. But the young turks of Cymdeithas yr Iaith, with Professor J.R.Jones as their guru, felt that self-respect demanded a militant and joyful opposition campaign in which Dafydd Iwan's satirical ballads were much sung. The investiture's adverse effect on Plaid Cymru was augmented by the six weeks show trial, costing £130,000, of Free Wales Army members, whose antics had been exploited by the establishment for years, aided by the subtle use of agents provocateurs, to discredit the political nationalists. The trial was brilliantly organised to close on the day of the investiture.

The second way of defusing nationalism was the time-honoured method of appointing a Royal Commission. Under the chairmanship first of Lord Crowther and then of Lord Kilbrandon, the Commission's immediate purpose was to buy time in the hope that the Welsh and Scots freedom movements would go away. Its establishment however was a remarkable tribute to Plaid Cymru. For the first time since the 1890's Welsh self-government was taken seriously by the London government. After agonising gestation the Labour Party gave evidence in favour of an elected assembly, though it would have no legislative powers. The Conservative Party, which was not threatened by Plaid

Cymru, declined to give evidence at all.

As for the Welsh M.P.'s, the majority persisted in their bitter opposition to any decentralisation of power, none more than George Thomas, the Secretary of State, who cynically exploited the IRA troubles. His constant contention was that if Wales had a parliament similar to Stormont, Wales like Northern Ireland would be engulfed in violence. Was not the IRA violence due to the existence of a parliament in the province? Did it not follow that a Welsh parliament would plunge Wales into a bloodbath? For the last 18 years the Northern Irish parliament has been closed down. Northern Ireland, like Wales, is governed directly from London. Yet so far from ceasing, violence in the Six Counties has continued at an even higher level than in the days of Stormont rule. London would give much to restore the province's parliament. George Thomas, Lord Tonypandy, is a colourful example of the lack of integrity of many opponents of Welsh self-government.

The Government's hope of using the Crowther/ Kilbrandon Commission as a window-dressing ploy until Wales' and Scotland's resurgent nationalism faded away seemed to be succeeding when both the Welsh and Scots nationalists lost their seats in 1970. However the establishment was again shocked when Emrys Roberts showed in the Merthyr Tydfil by-election of April 1972 that Welsh nationalism was still a force to be reckoned with by reducing the Labour majority from 17,655 in 1966 to 3,710. The Conservative candidate polled 7.3 per cent of the vote, the Communist 5.5 per cent and the Liberal 2.1 per cent. Four years later the nationalists gained control of the Merthyr Tydfil borough council together with the adjoining Rhymni Valley council.

The Kilbrandon Report, published in October 1973 at a time of renewed nationalist challenge, was a significant document. Six of the Commission's eleven members favoured a parliament with full legislative and tax-raising powers. The Conservative Party however, with very few exceptions, one being Edward Heath, was solidly opposed to decentralising any power, while the Labour Party lacked all enthusiasm. Scottish Labour was even more bitterly hostile than the Tories, fervently praying that nationalism would depart from the Scottish scene. They were soon disabused by Margo Macdonald's astonishing victory at Govan a week after the publication of the Kilbrandon Report. Fifteen years later her husband, Jim Sillars, was to win the same constituency for the SNP even more explosively.

1974 marked the biggest electoral advance yet for Welsh and Scottish nationalism. The SNP won six seats in the February election and Plaid Cymru two, losing Carmarthen by three votes. In the autumn Plaid Cymru increased its seats to three and the SNP to eleven. This had two extra-parliamentary consequences. Welsh Labour adopted the title The Labour Party in Wales in order to strengthen its Welsh identity. Much more important was the establishment of a TUC for Wales, thanks mainly to Dai Francis and Tom Jones, Shotton. Plaid Cymru's case for this, which had been pressed for a generation, was presented in an extensive pamphlet by Ithel Davies. Now the CBI is also organised on a national basis. Two decades earlier a group of nationalists had established Undeb Athrawon Cenedlaethol Cymru, the National Union of Welsh Teachers, and Welsh farmers had created their own independent union. Welsh national bodies were multiplying. The Welsh Arts Council had been set up in 1967, the Sports Council of Wales in 1972. The Welsh Books Council and Language Board strengthen Welsh literature and language, and the Welsh Academy and the Welsh Writers Union are a source of strength to scholars and writers in both Welsh and English. Professions such as doctors and bankers, solicitors and barristers now have their Welsh national organisations. National institutions are found in every field of activity, industry and commerce, culture and education, politics and administration, sport, radio and television. The University of Wales, the National Library, the National Museum and even the Church in Wales are major national institutions inherited from the days of Cymru Fydd nationalism. The splendid Folk Museum at St.Fagans, the fruit of the labours of another nationalist, Iorwerth Peate, is a more recent development. The National Eisteddfod, the nation's unique cultural festival, is far older than any of these, while the 6-day national youth Eisteddfod, organised by Urdd Gobaith Cymru, is an equally exciting institution in which thousands of children and young people compete.

The presence of 14 nationalists in parliament compelled the government reluctantly to move towards parliaments for Scotland and Wales. The pattern adopted for Wales was similar to that devised by Gwilym Prys Davies and supported by a Labour group led by James Griffiths. Included in a portmanteau bill for Scotland and Wales it came to grief early in 1977 because a number of Labour M.P.'s, including a group of Welshmen, either voted against it or abstained. Later in the year the Scotland Bill and the Wales Bill were introduced separately. The Wales Bill was debated for 29 days. The most vocal opposition came from the big group of hostile Welsh Labour M.P.'s led by Neil Kinnock and Leo Abse, who had the support of the London press and the *South Wales Echo*. Working in close cooperation with the Tories they were tightly organised with Donald Coleman and Ifor Davies acting as whips. Together with Scots and English Labour M.P.'s, particularly those from the envious north of England, they harassed the bill without let and with a freedom from discipline that indicated how little of the government's heart was in the bill. The prime minister, James Callaghan, was unconcerned; John Morris and Michael Foot were the only members of the cabinet to show any enthusiasm.

Although the proposed assembly was rather a pathetic affair it would have given Wales a national voice which could have been raised to effect during the barren Thatcher years, and could have ensured a fairer distribution of resources from the centre for economic development, housing and health, while a militant policy of job creation could have been pursued through the Welsh Development Agency. Most nationalists supported it because it would have given democratic control of the Welsh Office bureaucracy. For the first time Wales would have a democratic voice and a national political institution capable of dynamic development. The arguments deployed against it were largely specious. One which had a strong appeal in the wake of the unhappy local government reorganisation a few years earlier was that the assembly would add another tier of government, whereas it would in fact have democratised an already existing tier by assuming the extensive powers of the Welsh Office civil service. Much was made of the cost although it would have been less than the cost of S4C. A great deal was heard of the revealing complaint that the status of Westminster M.P.'s would be reduced because constituents would take their problems to assembly members. The slippery slope argument was a great favourite. If the Welsh people were allowed an elected assembly, the argument ran, they would demand more powers for it and slip all the way to full self-government. For Anglo British politicians it was unthinkable that the Welsh should govern themselves however right this was for the small Baltic nations or for the Basques and Catalans.

Ignorance of the nature of the proposed assembly was deep and widespread. It was quite commonly thought to be 'separatism', the hate-word so frequently used to whip up emotional antagonism. The confusion was extraordinary. Intelligent people did not distinguish between the assembly and Plaid Cymru's policy of full self-government. It was not known that Switzerland, with a tenth of Great Britain's population, had 26 canton governments, each with far more powers than the proposed assembly. Even a man of Leo Abse's intelligence could declare that the assembly would make Wales 'inward looking, losing connections and links with the whole of Britain.' For this undeviating centralist the slight measure of decentralisation proposed was 'tribalisation'. Abse's solution for excessive centralisation was a Welsh Select Committee. We've had one since 1980. Leo Abse was its first chairman. How many know of its existence? In what way has it modified London centralism or improved Welsh government?

The three Welsh nationalist M.P.'s pleaded time and again with Michael Foot, the leader of the House, for the government to inform the Welsh people of the powers of the assembly through publications and public statements by ministers, and that seminars and Saturday schools be organised by the Labour Party to enlighten its members. Although I went to see the prime minister with the same pleas next to nothing was done. Callaghan made only one speech on the matter. Neil Kinnock and Leo Abse were given a carte blanche to darken counsel and to frighten people. In the south-east they angered people with the spectre of rule by Welsh-speaking Gwynedd, while in Gwynedd, whose people voted massively against the assembly, the menace of the socialist south was invoked. Although these fears bore no relation to reality the establishment was happy to let confusion reign.

The background to the referendum was the social strife of the winter of discontent. Inflation had reached unprecedented heights, unemployment was rising fast, strikes multiplied, bodies were not being buried, rubbish remained uncollected. A Welsh elected assembly seemed an irritating irrelevance. Snow lay deep on the ground during the referendum campaign. The Conservative Party was solidly opposed, while Labour Party branches and Labour county council groups either abstained from support or actively opposed. The Llanelli branch was the sole exception in the south. County councillors generally feared that the assembly would abolish county councils. Lord Heycock, chairman of the Welsh County Councils Committee, declared that 'the way forward for Wales is the status quo'. Six only of the 23 Welsh Labour M.P.'s participated in the pro campaign. Dai Francis accused the Labour Party of 'organised sabotage'. The person who gained most in the assembly parliamentary debates and campaign was Neil Kinnock, whose able performance took him to the top of his party. Political expression of Welsh national identity is repugnant to him. His loyalty, he used to say, is given to his class. Justifying his opposition to a Welsh assembly in one of the 1978 devolution debates in the House of Commons, he declared confusingly,

> I believe that the emancipation of the class which I have come to this House to represent, unapologetically, can best be achieved in a single nation and a single economic unit, by which I mean a unit where we can have a brotherhood of all nations. . .

Since fighting for class is now unacceptable in a leader of the Labour Party his belief in class war has cooled, but his belief in a national future for his native country seems no warmer. His British nationalism is now unnalloyed by either class or Welsh loyalty.

The referendum result exceeded the fears of the most pessimistic of Welsh patriots. It demonstrated the extent of the success of the assimilation policy followed by English government since the 1536 Act of Incorporation. Saunders Lewis had said that the question implied in the referendum was whether Wales was a nation or not. He prophesied the consequences of a 'No' majority in this way:

> There will follow a general election. There may be a change of government. The first task of the new Westminster Parliament will be to reduce and master inflation. In Wales there are coalmines which work at

> a loss: there are steelworks that are judged super-
> fluous; there are still valleys convenient for submers-
> ion. And there will be no Welsh defence.

The experience of the Thatcher years in Wales was worse
than Saunders Lewis' prophecy. After the Welsh people
threw a minimal measure of self-rule back in London's
face, the Welsh nation was left defenceless against a
government which has the support of only seven of the 38
Welsh M.P.'s. This was of little account to the assembly's
opponents. When the referendum result was announced,
says John Osmond, civil servants at the Welsh Office broke
open bottles of champagne in an impromptu celebration
party. Bureaucrats had cause to rejoice; they would remain
free of democratic control.

Plaid Cymru had done its work. Getting the Wales Act
on the Statute Book was its biggest political achievement.
There was never a more bitter victory. After the demoralis-
ing referendum result the Act was repealed. But the government itself also paid a heavy price. It was brought down as a
consequence of the actions of Kinnock and the Labour
anti-devolutionists. The beneficiaries of the debacle were
the Tories. They alone could claim that they spoke for
Wales with a united voice on the matter of devolution.
Although the Conservative Party was again routed in
Wales in the general election, Mrs.Thatcher could do her
worst without hindrance from the Welsh. The three-
quarters of the Welsh people who opposed her were powerless. Therefore within months William Whitelaw declared in
Cambridge that the government would not honour its
pledge to establish a Welsh-language television channel.
After five years of Thatcherism Emlyn Williams, president
of the South Wales NUM, lamented that, 'Had we
devolution—a Welsh Assembly, a Parliament for Wales—
we would have had a voice.' Without an elected national
assembly the Welsh nation remained voiceless and
defenceless.

Despite this catastrophe Scottish and Welsh nationalism were now strong enough to guarantee that decentralisation and the democratisation of the countries of the United Kingdom would remain on the agenda. Then came an astonishing development which is bound to help to transform the Welsh situation. Great Britain was the most highly centralised state in the European Community, but east European states and the Soviet republics were even more centralist. Then suddenly in 1989 centralism was peacefully swept away even in eastern Europe and the Baltic republics. Democratic nationalism created democracies in Estonia, Latvia, Lithuania, Poland, East Germany, now unified with West Germany, Czechoslovakia and Hungary, leaving Great Britain the most highly centralised state in Europe.

This democratic revolution has left the British order untouched. No eddies have disturbed the Welsh backwater up to now. The Conservative Party has not yet considered any move towards a more decentralist and democratic order. The Labour Party has published a pathetic policy for Wales which will be implemented if a Labour government gets round to reorganising local and regional government in England. This policy, which would give Wales equality of status with the West Midlands region, is outlined in a document significantly entitled *A Statement on the Future of Local and Regional Government.* In its ten pages the document uses the words 'region' and 'regional' in relation to Wales 49 times. The word 'nation' is conspicuous by its absence. Centralism, underpinned by Anglo British nationalism, reigns supreme.

A victim of the amazing pace of events in Europe, the idea of a Soviet nation, which corresponds to the British 'nation', has collapsed. Unlike British nationalism, the Soviet nationalism to which Stalin appealed with such effect during the war, is no more. The Moscow government will soon have no power in Estonia, Latvia, Lithuania and other nations of the Russian empire. It was Estonia, half the size of Wales, which did most to initiate the process of democratisation of countries in the USSR on the basis of nationhood. But while nationalist movements have done so much to give new hope and vitality to many nations in eastern Europe and the Russian empire, Wales, which was a nation 1200 years before Great Britain came into existence, remains wholly subject to the centralist London government, without a shred of national freedom, still locked in the British 'nation' and soaked in British nationalism. This outrageous situation must be faced as a challenge. The stranglehold of London can only be broken by a nationalism as powerful as that which cast off Moscow rule and Soviet nationalism in Estonia. As an Estonian democracy has been created so must we create a Welsh democracy. Will the Welsh people rise to the level of history?

15 / A Free Wales in a European Confederation

THE BREATH-TAKING changes of the European revolution, in which nationalism and democracy are so closely interwoven, cannot fail in time to transform the Welsh political situation. Welsh nationalists, who think of themselves as Welsh Europeans, can be the catalyst of a fundamental change which, with Scottish nationalism, will lead to the democratisation of the countries in Britain. The nationalism of the small Baltic countries, which has played such a noble part in taking perestroika to its logical limits in the Russian empire, has been strikingly relevant to Wales, while the democratising of Czechoslovakia by Czech nationalists, whose great liberator after the first world war, Tomaš Masaryk, a distinguished exponent of moderate democratic nationalism, was a hero of the first generation of Welsh nationalists, has been a particular inspiration.

There has been a sea-change in the context in which we work. Great Britain now has the look of an imperial Victorian relic. The only case for the preservation of the Great British power state is the narrow Anglo-British nationalist one. No valid case can be made from the European or world standpoint or from the Welsh or Scottish standpoint for huge centralist power states. The days of centralist English control of Wales are drawing to an end, though with depressing sluggishness. As long as they continued unquestioned it was reasonable to contend, though Plaid Cymru never did, that devolution or federalism was an adequate answer to the Welsh national question.

However events have moved with such staggering speed that devolution and federalism, giving the Welsh and Scots some control of their domestic affairs, look passé, suited to the age before the European revolution. The new European situation requires that English oppression in Wales, which is a basic fact however benign the oppression, must be completely removed. Devolution barely touches the situation. It belongs to the pre-Gorbachev past, to the age when the Welsh thought it right and important to defend Great Britain's great power status. That era has ended. Devolving some power from London to Wales is no more an answer now than devolving some power from Moscow to Estonia or Lithuania. All power over the life of Wales must be transferred to the Welsh people as all power over Estonian life is being transferred to the Estonian people. Just as the small Baltic nations are ending Russian rule so must Wales end English rule. Just as they now enjoy full national status so must the ancient nation of Wales, whose future as an equal lies among the peoples of Europe.

Welsh nationalists were taught by Saunders Lewis, whose splendid essay on Tomaš Masaryk is still remembered, to see Wales as a European nation, and Welsh civilisation as a part of the civilisation of Europe 'To bring political and economic unity to Europe,' said Lewis in 1927, 'should be one of the first priorities of our century.' Although it is far more than the sum of its parts, European civilisation, which is its great glory, is not an abstraction hovering above Europe. It is composed of the cultures of scores of nations and historic regions, each making its unique contribution. Its incomparable richness lies in the diversity to which many nations, Wales not least among them, have contributed irrespective of size. The foundations of European civilisation were laid by the small peoples of Greece and Israel. The Renaissance flowered in the small independent Italian city-states, especially Florence, Milan and Venice. The great musicians of the

18th and 19th century, such as Beethoven and Bach, Handel and Haydn, Mendelssohn and Wagner were born in small independent German states, Mozart in the city-state of Salzburg. The huge German power state created by Bismarck produced no musician of comparable stature or civilisation of comparable quality. The population of Shakespeare's England was little bigger than Wales today.

The hope of a national future for Wales lies in her becoming an equal member of the European Community. The people of Wales must learn to think of themselves not as British but as Welsh Europeans, members of the international community. Raymond Williams showed the way when he declared himself to be,

> 'a Welsh European. I want the Welsh people—still a radical and cultured people—to defeat, override or bypass bourgeois England. That connects, for me, with the sense in my work that I am now necessarily European. . .'

When the western Roman Empire fell Wales was the only land which had been a part of it to remain unconquered, except for the Basque country. It therefore remained Christian when the Franks and Saxons overran northern Gaul, England and southern Scotland. This enabled the Welsh saints to help relight the lamps of Christianity in northwestern Gaul in the first positive Welsh contact with the life of continental Europe. Welsh saints were among the leaders of the settlement of Brittany. Wales was the epicentre of the great missionary effort which spread by the western sea-routes to Iceland and to Spain, and which we think of as Celtic Christianity. P.A.Wilson says that although it was in Ireland that the Celtic Church achieved its greatest renown, the initial impetus came from sub-Roman Britain. A number of the greatest scholars of the age were British, including Pelagius, Faustus, Fastidius and the Sicilian Briton. Patrick too was a Brythonic-speaking Briton. Their first language was Brythonic, from which

Welsh developed in the Age of Saints, during which Wales herself developed as a national community. The supreme Welsh contribution to European civilisation was made six centuries later with the Arthurian romances which helped to raise the status of women and, so Renan contends, inaugurated the movement of chivalry. These were composed near the time of the Norman invasion. 'The Normans made the Welsh a European people', says Professor Gwyn Alf Williams. 'They prized Wales out of the Celtic-Scandinavian world of the Irish Sea and incorporated it into Latin Europe.'

When M.Tindemans, Prime Minister of Belgium, came to Cardiff on 2 July 1975 during his tour of inquiry into European union, he was met by Plaid Cymru representatives who presented him with a document which stated the party's three aims: (i) to secure self-government for Wales, (ii) to play a full role as a nation in international affairs, and (iii) to restore the economic and cultural life of Wales; and then declared,

> The party has always been profoundly aware of Wales' place in European civilisation. Plaid Cymru has therefore sought to restore and maintain Welsh civilisation, and has regarded self-government as a necessary means of achieving this. The party has always campaigned for 'self-government' and 'freedom' for Wales—rather than absolute independence or sovereignty.

From its foundation the Welsh national party has had a lively consciousness of Wales as a European nation. We rejoice that today, after half a century of Americanisation, Europe and its civilisation are being rediscovered. In particular the small stateless nations and historic regions are taking a new pride in their European roots and native culture and moving towards full political autonomy. The day of the great highly centralised power states, which have so long divided Europe and plunged it into bloody wars, is coming to an end. The elephantine centralist Anglo British state which for so long kept the Celtic nations of the British Isles submerged in marginalised peripheral regions, is an anachronism, a political dinosaur. Before long economic separatism between states and nations will be swept away by freedom of movement for people, goods and capital, unhindered by passports or visas, tariffs or tolls. This is not wholly good but it has the great advantage that the military and economic factors which gave birth to and sustained huge centralised states will be no more. In the developing situation the Welsh nation can confidently hope to emerge from its obscurity and servitude to live its own life fully and to play an active part in European life. From being passive spectators of the European scene the Welsh can become creative participants. Wales can become a foundation member of the new Europe, helping to mould the future order. This is the objective for which Plaid Cymru campaigns.

Outside Great Britain there is an increasing awareness that huge centralised states retard economic and cultural development, that smallness can be an economic and cultural advantage. The history of the Baltic nations illustrates this. Sweden, which has always enjoyed national freedom, is with Switzerland the most successful country in Europe. Incorporated in Russia until 1918-20, Finland, Estonia, Latvia and Lithuania were backward countries, but, winning freedom after the first world war, all four developed amazingly. Then Estonia, Latvia and Lithuania were once more incorporated in the Russian empire. Their development was reversed, while Finland, smaller than Scotland, despite comparative poverty of natural resources, became one of the most thriving countries in the world, culturally and economically. Norman Macrae has, with no more than a touch of exaggeration, taken the advantages of smallness further:

> Of the 15 republics in the Soviet Disunion, up to 14 intend to secede. When these are 15 separate

republics, parts of most will also wish to break away as separate countries or cantons. This could be a recipe for prosperity rather than chaos. Economically, India might have done better after independence to split into a hundred Hong Kongs. Things would certainly have gone worse if India had been kept gummed in a single union with Pakistan and Bangladesh.

Had Wales enjoyed Finland's freedom its condition might be comparable with Finland's today. But 'kept gummed in a single union' with England the Welsh nation is in ruin.

There will be a warm welcome in Europe for Wales, whose capital city of Cardiff was the first capital of a stateless nation in which the EEC placed an office. Not only is there little love for Great Britain among European nations, there is a growing awareness that in the fully integrated Europe so deeply desired, its splendid diversity must be fully recognised and fostered. This recognition was formally stated in a Joint Declaration by the European Green Parties: 'The diversity of its cultures, of its peoples and regions, is one of Europe's greatest assests, to be conserved and developed for the benefit of every European.' The Green Party of Wales has recognised the essential role of political nationalism. 'The nationalism of the small nations is a cry for self-determination instead of colonial status. It is a cry for free expression and cultural and political diversity, instead of externally imposed uniformity.' The European Parliament itself showed its recognition of the need to safeguard cultural diversity in a resolution passed by an overwhelming majority in November 1988 calling for the establishment of elected assemblies with law-making powers for the European regions, with sufficient resources to manage their own affairs and with direct access to the European Community institutions—what Plaid Cymru had been pressing for since the U.K. entered the common market.

The submerged nations and historic regions are a vitally

valuable element in the diversity which enriches European civilisation. The increasing interdependence of nations in Europe is matched by a growing awareness of the value of diverse identities. Some, like Euzkadi, Catalonia and Flanders have recently achieved a measure of self-government; all of them have their own history and culture; many have their own languages. The half a million people who speak Welsh are not odd people in the European context. On average each of the twelve members of the European Community has two lesser-used but distinctive languages as well as that spoken by the majority of the population. Fifty million people speak languages which are not the language of the State. This large and powerful lobby within the Community is becoming strongly organised on a European basis. Since John Hume introduced the resolution which led to the Arfe Report, the European Parliament has devoted considerable time to the question of minority languages, and a number of meetings have been held with the Commission in Brussels to discuss the matter. An important consequence has been the establishment of the European Bureau for Lesser Used Languages with a secretariat in Dublin, a recognition of the leadership given by the Irish.

This European language movement enables those who fight for their languages, all of them concerned with the link between language and national sense of identity, to escape from the suffocation of the dominant culture in their state. Although Wales has no representation in any European institution Welsh nationalists are in the forefront of the language struggle on the European level. A notable success has been the establishment of the first European centre for lesser used languages at Nant Gwrtheyrn in Gwynedd. The Welsh language is an increasingly close link between Wales and Europe, particularly with the 50 million who speak the lesser used languages.

The lack of fair representation for stateless nations and historic regions is a deep flaw in the EEC. The Welsh position is absurdly unjust. Luxembourg, a people without a literature, the population of Gwent, has a member on the Council of Ministers, the most powerful body in the institution, has the right to nominate a member of the Commission, and has six members in the European Parliament. Wales, an old European nation with a population of 2¾ millions, has never been represented on the Council of Ministers, has no right to nominate a Commissioner, and has only four members of the European Parliament. If Wales had full national status it would have representation on the Council of Ministers and the Commission and 15 MEP's, as Ireland has.

Its exclusion from Brussels has cost Wales dear. The milk quotas scandal is a striking example. When they were discussed by the Council of Ministers there was no one present to speak for Wales despite the great importance of milk to Welsh farmers. Wales was represented by Jopling, the English minister of agriculture, the very man who was pressing for more quotas. Consequently Welsh milk quotas were twice drastically slashed, driving many farmers out of business, severely reducing the incomes of many more and causing the closure of Welsh creameries in areas of high unemployment. Every business dependent on agriculture suffered. In Ireland quotas were raised. Irish farmers had a member on the Council of Ministers to fight their case. In 1989 an Irishman became the Commissioner for Agriculture. In 1990 the Irish Prime Minister, Charles Haughey, became President of the Council of Ministers. There is no one to remind this powerful governing body of the existence of Wales.

The injustice suffered by Welsh milk farmers has been echoed in the case of sheep. Sheep are immensely important to Welsh agriculture; no less than 17 per cent of the European sheep population is in Wales. Who represented Wales in the vitally important sheep negotiations? None other then John Gummer, who came close to doing a Jopling.

Consequently Welsh hill farmers may face a bleaker future than even the dairy farmers. The position is scandalous. The Council of Ministers meets 70 times a year. Ministers from Ireland and Luxembourg attend all meetings. The Secretary of State for Wales has never attended. The case for full national status, which alone will give Wales representation on the institutions of the EEC, is irrefutable.

Wales has no kind of presence in Brussels, not even a delegation to lobby for Welsh interests. Every one of the fifteen länder governments of Germany has a full delegation there. Yet no party but Plaid Cymru has fought for Welsh representation in Brussels. The Labour Party, the establishment party in Wales, has never given it a thought. The reason is that Labour thinks of Wales not as a nation but as a region, on a level with the English East Midlands. Labour's regional Welsh policy has no place for a direct relationship between Wales and the European Community although this is undeniably an urgent Welsh need.

In Europe however Plaid Cymru does not fight alone. It is an active member of the European Free Alliance, a grouping of 20 parties from such countries as Flanders and Euzkadi, Alsace and Brittany, Ireland and Scotland, who share our aims and values. The Alliance's 14 MEP's belong to the colourful Rainbow Group which has full group status in the European Parliament. In active contact with the German Greens and other environmental parties it constantly raised issues concerning the environment, the eradication of poverty, human rights, including the right to self-determination, and nuclear and conventional disarmament.

The interests of peripheral Wales require a dual movement. On the one hand the nation must become more closely integrated in Europe with a place in the Brussels decision-making process on a basis of equality with other nations. It should be represented in the Council of Ministers, the Commission and the important committees, and there should be a fairer representation in the European Parliament. This would be undeniably beneficial, but it is not possible until the Welsh people achieve self-government, giving them the power in Wales herself to develop the Welsh economy on the basis of nationhood. Neither an equal place in Europe nor the power to develop a balanced economy is possible without full national status. Full self-government is therefore the condition of the future welfare of the Welsh nation. A devolved or federal Welsh government would neither give Wales membership in the European Community nor full power to create a balanced economy.

European economic development will inevitably tend to be concentrated in the London-Paris-Frankfurt-Amsterdam area, which includes the 'home counties' and the whole region within a hundred miles of London. Only a Welsh government would implement a policy which would effectively counter the consequences of this in Wales, and a Welsh government alone would press vigorously for the adequate recognition of Wales in an effective regional policy designed to rectify economic disparities.

Although Welsh nationalists have been constantly derided in the past as separatists the political freedom they envisaged never entailed economic separation. Now, in the European common market, economic separation is impossible even for the biggest countries. Germany will be as closely woven as Luxembourg into European economic life. The economies of all members of the EEC are becoming increasingly inter-dependent. After 1992 passports will be unnecessary between them, tariffs and tolls will be non-existent, frontiers will have lost their meaning. Therefore the strongest objection raised against Welsh self-government in the past is disappearing completely. Today's Welsh separatists are those who want to keep Wales separate from Europe.

The constitution of the European Community is far from

being ideal. It needs to be democratised and decentralised, and the whole of Europe needs to be demilitarised, freed of Nato as well as the Warsaw Pact. However it is in the process of development; its character, even its size, are not finally decided. It could take a form harmful to Wales, making self-government even more necessary. There is a danger that the big states will forge the Community wholly in their own interests and the interests of the giant companies concentrated in the central golden bloc. Because market forces are a centralising phenomenon the economically dominant central bloc could wield decisive political power, just as the economically dominant southeast of England does in the British state. The extension of the Community to include countries as far as Estonia is most desirable, but it would marginalise a stateless Wales still further. The shift of power to the centre could lead, in the absence of powerful decentralising pressures to a federal state with overmuch power in the central government which would be used in the interests of the biggest states. That is always a danger in federalism.

The dangers that lie in hugeness have often been demonstrated. So have the virtues of smallness. The countries enjoying the most advanced social policies, the lowest unemployment and the highest level of aid to the third world are the small countries that belong to EFTA, Norway, Sweden, Iceland, Austria and Switzerland, with Finland an associate member. Their success owes much to their small size.

Fortunately, if there is a shift to the centre there is also a counter-shift towards the regions, towards a decentralist confederal Europe. A Europe of 50 or more nations and historic regions would have to be more democratic and decentralised than the 'Europe of the Twelve'. European decentralism would obviously be strengthened by Welsh self-government, but we must do all we can to further it today. The Welsh are not alone. They have allies among the tens of stateless nations and historic regions in Europe, many of which share the Welsh experience of living under state systems which are injurious to their cultural and economic life. Together in the European Free Alliance, whose members have an instinctive understanding of the Welsh condition, Wales and other small nations have a little leverage in moving the new Europe in the right direction. Just as Scots and Welsh nationalists are in the vanguard of the process of democratising the countries of the United Kingdom so is the European Free Alliance in the van of the movement to create a decentralised confederal Europe rather than a federal Europe with an overstrong central government. Welsh nationalists identify with Willy Kuijpers, the great Flemish nationalist, who declared,

> The worst thing that can happen to a nation is to live in isolation. But this doesn't mean that we have to create a monolithic Europe. If we leave Europe to big business, we'll soon be eating plastic hamburgers from Oslo to Madrid. Therefore we must fight centralism and demand respect for the rights of peoples. Small nations can contribute to peace on the basis of non-alliance with the superpowers.

The growth of national consciousness and a strong sense of identity in the small nations and historic regions of Europe helps to ensure that the status quo will not be set in concrete and that a shift towards centralism is preventable. It can grow strong enough to provide a lever to loosen the order in the way that the nationalisms of Estonia, Latvia and Lithuania, two of which are smaller than Wales, became the lever which cracked the centralism of the huge totalitarian Russian empire. It was their will to freedom which fuelled this amazing development. Their right to freedom is no greater than that of Wales but their will to achieve it is infinitely greater.

The Europe for which Welsh nationalists work is a partnership of free and equal nations in a nuclear-free confederal order, in which there will be a strong regional policy to counterbalance the adverse effects of market forces. The European Parliament would have legislative powers and would include a second chamber in which the nations and historic regions are represented. Many of the the functions of the Council of Ministers, which currently controls the EC, would be transferred to this second chamber. We look to a decentralist diversified Europe of many nations, peoples and historic regions, each with its own beating heart, a Europe in which power would be retained as locally as possible. No nation would be subordinate to another.

Two advantages of such a loose confederation are that countries, such as those of the Baltic and eastern Europe, might accede to it more easily, and that anti-democratic elements would find it impossible to gain control over it. This is the road to true European integration and to a flourishing European civilisation. Whereas huge centralist states, whose priorities have been power and military prestige, cause deep divisions, the supple cooperation of a big number of nations and regions of all sizes is the way to deeper unity and a richer civilisation. Diversity is the condition of deep integration. The real advocates of integration are those who work for a Europe united in all the richness of its diversity.

In this Europe of the nations and historic regions the Welsh nation has a natural place, but it is still locked in the vice of the huge centralist British state, which is possessed by a yearning for greatness, as its immense armaments budget and its monstrous nuclear weapons testify. Increasingly it looks incongruous and rather ridiculous at this time of breath-taking revolutionary change in Europe, when the power of nationalism has peacefully democratised country after country. Wales however, incorporated in fossilised Great Britain, is stuck in a time warp, stationary, static, stagnant, with no more power over her national life than she had 100 years ago.

National freedom is the condition of Welsh national survival. If we don't put an end to our servitude, our servitude will put an end to us. The role of Welsh nationalism is to mobilise Welsh people power to take the Welsh nation into her natural European home. If the people of Wales act with dignified resolution to create a Welsh state, the great possibilities that lie latent in this talented little nation can yet enrich the civilisation of Europe.

Other stimulating political books published by Y Lolfa:

THE INNER CITY
Leopold Kohr   £4.95
Why do cities grow and decay? Why is all
bureaucratic planning doomed to failure? Why
is so much architecture rubbish?—a brilliant,
iconoclastic, entertaining new book by the
originator of the "small is beautiful"
philosophy. He contrasts the Inner City of
today that is besieged by uncontrollable social
and economic problems with the ideal, convivial
Inner City catering for a variety of human-sized
needs.
0 86243 177 8

THE CELTIC REVOLUTION
Peter Berresford Ellis   £4.95
A comprehensive, up-to-date, pan-Celtic primer
surveying the histories and cultures of the six
Celtic nations and examining their current
political prospects; now reprinted.
0 86243 096 8

THE ABC OF THE WELSH REVOLUTION
Derrick Hearne   £3.95
An ambitious work proposing a new, radical
nationalist ideology and describing life in
independent Welsh Community Benefit State to
be established at the turn of the century. Essential, stimulating reading for all thinking
Welshmen. 288 pp.
0 86243 015 1